PITTSBURGH ORIGINAL TEXTS AND
TRANSLATION SERIES

Dikran Y. Hadidian

General Editor

1

SELECTED WRITINGS OF HANS DENCK

SELECTED WRITINGS OF HANS DENCK

EDITED AND TRANSLATED FROM THE TEXT

As Established by

WALTER FELLMANN

By

EDWARD J. FURCHA
SERAMPORE COLLEGE
SERAMPORE, INDIA

With

FORD LEWIS BATTLES
Pittsburgh Theological Seminary

THE PICKWICK PRESS
PITTSBURGH, PENNSYLVANIA
1975

Library of Congress Cataloging in Publication Data

Denck, Johannes, 1495(ca.)-1527.
    Selected writings of Hans Denck.

    (Pittsburgh original texts and translations series ;
1)
    Translation of Exegetische Schriften.
    Includes bibliographical references and index.
    1. Anabaptists--Collected works. 2. Theology--
Collected works--16th century. I. Title.
BX4929.D4613   230'.4'3   76-7057
ISBN 0-915138-15-8

TABLE OF CONTENTS

Preface

Denck has been an enigma to students of sixteenth century Protestantism. He is generally found next to Th. Muentzer, Sebastian Franck and Caspar von Schwenckfeld among extreme representatives of the left wing or else, described as a spiritualist reformer. Then again, he is counted among Anabaptists of the day.

His Upper Bavarian homeland possibly accounts for the fact that he has often been mentioned in connection with Balthasar Hubmaier. Whether or not one is prepared to connect the two men by the link of baptism, as has generally been done, it should be apparent after cursory investigation even that marked differences in personality and teaching distinguish the two, despite the claim by their contemporary U. Rhegius of Augsburg that they are the two major representatives of the "baptismal order."

G.H.Williams maintains that a certain dependence by Hubmaier on some of Denck's tenets is evident in Humbaier's second booklet on free will (1527). We cannot here go into details of the relationship and must rest content by stating that there is an unmistakable affinity of thought regarding theological essentials despite dissimilarities in emphasis and direction.

Unfortunately, Denck's own writings provide rather scant evidence for extensive analysis of this kind. They fill no more than two slender volumes in the critical edition of his work by Walter Fellmann in the series QUELLEN UND FORSCH UNGEN ZUR REFORMATIONSGESCHICHTE (1956, 1960).

Fellmann divided Denck's work in two categories, the religious and exegetical works respectively. Except for some letters and a few poems nothing else seems to have survived to our day from the life of a man whose career showed the promise of brilliance yet who stood obscured for all too long by the magnitude of the giants of his age on whom the attention of scholars has been focused primarily.

Motivated by developments in the twentieth century and by an awakened interest in revolutionaries, renewed pre-occupation with the personalities in the radical wing of the reformation period has brought Hans Denck and his aims to the fore once again.

We feel that a translation of the work of this seminal thinker is long overdue so that English speaking students may avail themselves at first hand of the ideas of this Christian scholar. Admittedly, one of his writings is already available in English. This has not been included here. Nor has it been feasible to translate Denck's work on the prophet Micah.

The translated material, however, has been arranged in three sections to cover three prominent phases of the Reformer's work. Part I gives excerpts from his interaction with contemporary reformers and churchmen, showing him in theological dialogue. In Part II we have translated three documents from among his theological writings. Part III contains a statement which reflects the final break with Anabaptist tenets. The total literary output spans hardly more than two or three years from about 1524-1527. Appended in Part IV is He who _truly_ _loves_ _the_ _Truth_, Denck's _Paradoxa_.

As we follow Denck through his most productive
years, we catch a glimpse of the inner tensions
that make of him an evangelical reformer at one
point, an ardent Anabaptist at another and an advocate of "spiritual" Christianity (understood in
the Troeltschian sense of that term), at the apex
of his short yet fruitful and exciting life.

The framework of this life is quickly given.
Denck is said to have been born in 1500.   In
November 1527 he succumbed to the plague.   This
short life was filled, however, with the attainment
of a good humanist education, a varied career in
proof reading, teaching and literary pursuits.

As early as 1521 Denck seems to have been
attracted to Reform ideas during a time in Regens-
burg where he was then teaching.   Through the good
offices of Oecolampadius, the Reformer of Basel, he
was able to secure in 1523 the post of Rektor of
the St. Sebaldschule in Nuernberg.

In this city undoubtedly he deepened his ties
with the reform movement.   It was here also that
Denck made his fullest acquaintance with Anabaptist
and Radical tenets.   Wittingly or otherwise he was
drawn into disputes with Osiander, senior preacher,
and eventually with the City Fathers.   By 1525 he
had lost his post.   He was forced, as a result, to
spend the remaining two years of his life "on the
road," as it were.

Two documents from the Nuernberg period are
of particular interest to us.   They are Denck's own

Confession and the official Evaluation of it, presented to the City Fathers by a group of evangelical
preachers in the City.

By the time Denck's Confession reached these
men, his name or notoriety must have long preceded
the document. A brief analysis bears out this
observation, for the Evaluation by the preachers
shows clearly that they must have responded to a
caricature of the man rather than to specific matters he stated in the document.
Next to the so-called Recantation (1528), none
of Denck's extant writings is more carefully phrased
or more irenic in tone than this "enforced confession" on the basis of which he was to be proved
"catholic."

He begins the Confession with an expression of
creature feeling, acknowledging the sense of futility which seems to have overcome his sensitive
nature in face of the internal warfare between good
and evil. Not unlike Luther--who despaired of the
inability of good works in restoring a person to
wholesomeness and inward peace--Denck knows of the
limitation of Scripture in itself. He discovers
truth to be the driving force within him which
alone can make Scripture meaningful. Neither
learning nor self-confidence can accomplish such
a task. In fact, Denck blames Scripture for being
a source of faction and darkness, if taken as its
own interpreter. Almost predictably, one can
expect in response a virulent defence by protagonists
of the sola scriptura principle.

Denck is willing to be tested on five counts, namely his understanding of Scripture, sin, the righteousness of God, the Law and the Gospel. However, for reasons of brevity (or was it a genuine desire "not to offend anyone or disparage anything"?), he says little about sin and rests content by stating that Law and Gospel are executed by Christ "as king of righteousness."

Although he had intended not to express himself on Baptism and the Eucharist he does so in a statement which occupies roughly as much space again as he had devoted to the above-mentioned items. What he says on Baptism could hardly have endeared him either to the Lutherans or to the Anabaptists of the day. He minimizes the significance of water baptism by suggesting instead that "an inward baptism" is necessary unto salvation.

Repeatedly Denck returns to the theme of his unworthiness and inward pollution. Because of this "natural" state even the eating of bread and the drinking from the Cup in Communion can be harmful to a sinful man, unless he is able to advance by the gracious intervention of God to an invisible communion. How much of the Crautwald-Schwenckfeld spirit has he imbibed? Or, to raise a prior question, how much of this stance is inspired by the mysticism of Tauler?

The verdict by the preachers sheds some light, it would seem, not so much on the degree of Denck's heretical utterances, as it does on the precarious position he had put himself in by being a maverick

of evangelical Christianity in his disregard for
some of the pillars of Luther's system.

With some irony, the preachers admit Denck's
brilliance ("Scripture never speaks as pointedly
as he does," they state). What they eventually
make of his speaking pointedly is, of course, a
different matter.

They begin--after the usual courteous prelimin-
aries--by accusing him of devious answers. This
point is followed immediately by another ad hominem
argument on the purity of his motives. They find
it hard to follow his line which employs paradox
(a favorite method of Sebastian Franck also), to a
arrive at truth. His alleged high-handed treatment of Scripture is attacked, in the third place.
The evaluators obviously failed to see that Denck
did not intend to demolish the authority of Scripture but rather to place it in proper perspective
as that which points to the Word but is not itself
the Word.

Point by point the Evaluation scores with
heavy hand what in the opinion of these representatives of the Lutheran cause should have been said
yet was not made explicit by Denck. In the end,
one is left with the distinct impression that a
genuine dialogue on the matters at issue had not
taken place at all.

Denck had, of course, spoken guardedly,
possibly to avoid pitfalls. This economy of
words is now used against him as if his silence
were a tacit admission of a faulty position.

Their report then sounds more like a prosecutor's
brief than an objective evaluation. It is hardly
surprising that a troublemaker of such dark pigmen-
tation had to be dismissed from his post as Rektor
and banned from the City.

Does the Recantation, written two years later
and under somewhat more favorable circumstances
reveal anything further about the theological
stance of Hans Denck? It covers ten items of
Christian faith. Oddly enough, Denck is silent
on the doctrine of God, says little on Christology
except for a brief statement on atonement, and
nothing on pneumatology and the last things. A
doctrine of the Church is implied only in a short
statement on sects. Undoubtedly the reformer saw
no need of speaking on matters on which he considered himself well within Catholic teaching.

Starting with Scripture--the declared authority
of the evangelical Reformers--Denck reiterates a
position he had maintained earlier, namely that
Scripture is not the Word of God. Nor does he
find Scripture conducive to salvation unless a
person has already been chosen by God before he is
exposed to the reading or hearing of Scripture.
The principle here propounded is definitely against
Luther's own view. It does, however, find echoes
in the work of Sebastian Franck (who is even more
extreme), and in that of Caspar von Schwenckfeld.
One gets the impression though, that Denck does not
at all intend to depreciate Scripture. On the contrary, he seems to search for a way around the
problem of how the illiterate masses might receive

salvation. In view of the large numbers of
illiterate and semi-literate people in his day,
this stance is not only highly laudable but certainly most charitable.

Denck continues to affirm the sinlessness of
believers in Christ. Again, unlike Luther he conceives of free will as inevitable in view of the
compelling nature of divine love. However, the
argument pro and con is judged by him unworthy of
controversy since liberation for service is according to him all that ultimately counts.

Similarly, he disapproves of any coercion in
matters of faith. Like Schwenckfeld and Sebastian
Franck, he seeks to advocate a spiritual fellowship with all those "who hold high the wondrous
deed of God through Christ."   One looks in vain
for a high doctrine of the Church as either "body
of Christ" or "vicar of Christ." This lack is
confirmed by Denck's view on ceremonies and sacraments (Sections vii and viii).

On Baptism he speaks with the same disregard
for the outward practice which Schwenckfeld had
shown in his "Stillstand" on the Lord's Supper.[10]
He is prepared to give up baptism if that should
prove to be God's will. Advocacy of spiritual
communion and a firm stand against the swearing of
oaths complete this document which, if not offen-
sive in any of its major tenets, certainly does
not allow either for any definitive conclusion about
Denck's theological frame of mind at the end of
his life.

In Reformation histories Denck has been given
numerous labels. To some scholars he appeared a

"contemplative Anabaptist."   Other accounts tend
to make of him a protagonist of undogmatic churchmanship.   In the extensive and thoroughgoing
studies of Rufus Jones, F.L.Weiss and A.Coutts he
appears to be a Quaker, a Unitarian and a Humanist
respectively.   We are not about to provide an
additional category even though one might rightly
call for a renewed assessment of the man and his
work. Let his writings speak for themselves.

     In defence of the man it should be said, how-
ever, that he appears to have been a singularly
"private person," despite the notoriety in the
ecclesiastical circles of his day which has made
subsequent objective judgment difficult. We know
next to nothing of his family background. He
shunned controversy as an end in itself yet could
not fully escape engagement in the issues of his
day. His views on the nature of man and the manner
in which he viewed opposing forces within himself
testify to an introspective trend in his nature.
Fanaticism or showmanship do not seem to have been
characteristic of Denck. Yet he was feared as an
enthusiast and forced to live in humble circumstances on the sidelines of momentous developments
in Central Europe.

     This selection makes no claim of completeness
in covering Denck's writings or views. We offer
the following excerpts from the Reformer's pen in
the hope that contemporary readers will give them
the attention they deserve and perchance recognize
in them "Christ the mediator whom no one can truly
know, except he follow him in his own life"(Was

<u>Geredt</u> <u>sei</u> <u>dass</u> <u>die</u> <u>Schrift</u> <u>sagt</u>, Fellmann,
<u>Schriften</u>, 2.Teil, p.45).

July, 1975

Serampore College   Edward J. Furcha
Serampore, W.B., India

Editor's Note.

I wish to express my thanks to Mr. Edward Sieger of Pitts-burgh, who typed the book in final form.

August, 1975
Norwich, Vermont, USA   *Ford Lewis Battles*

I.1

H. Denck

CONFESSION ADDRESSED TO THE
CITY COUNCIL OF NUERNBERG
(1525)

Schriften, 2.Teil, pp.20-26

Note:

During the fall of 1523 the City Council of
Nuernberg decided to support Luther's reform
efforts. In order to do so effectively, a united
endeavour seemed desirable. Hence theologically
well trained men such as the priest Andreas
Osiander were engaged to silence dissenting voices.
Even prominent men and their circles, such as the
Duerer group, were not exempt from careful scrutiny.
Among these the Behaim brothers especially soon
became known as the "godless painters" and were
accused of disregarding communion, taking Scripture
lightly and holding Christ for naught.

Denck had just accepted the post of principal
of the St. Sebald Gymnasium, a prominent high
school in Nuernberg. He was therefore quickly
drawn into the circle of those whose religious
stance was suspect.

In January 1525 Denck was called before the
Council to defend his views. Partly because of the
weakness of the accusations, partly because of his
skill, he was able to hold his own. The preachers
of Nuernberg, charged with probing the orthodoxy
of his faith, had to admit that Denck handled himself
so well that any further oral cross examination
would prove futile. Hence Denck was ordered to
submit his views in writing on seven essential
points of Christian doctrine and practice. Denck
responded and presented his "statement of faith"
later in January in two separate submissions. The
first submission deals with the nature of faith in

a general way, while Part II, submitted before
20 January 1525, covers Denck's views pertaining to
Baptism and the Lord's Supper. The City Fathers
were to make their decision on the basis of an
evaluation by the preachers of Nuernberg (see our
second selection).

Meanwhile, Denck impatiently and somewhat
indiscreetly had his Confession circulated in the
town. As a result he was asked to leave town
immediately.[1]

Confession addressed to the City
Council of Nuernberg, 1525

I.

I, John Denck, confess that I truly find,
feel, and sense myself to be a pitiable man by
birth; a man who is subject to every disease of
body and soul.

However, I also feel within me something that
strongly opposes my natural obstinate nature and
points me to a life or blessedness which appears as
impossible for my soul to attain as it seems impossible for my body to climb up into the visible sky.

It is said that faith leads to life. I'll
accept that. But who gives me this faith? If it
were inborn in me, I should have this life by
birth; this is not so, however.

Since childhood I have learned the faith from
my parents and uttered it with my mouth. Later I

read it in men's books. Moreover, I boasted of my
faith. In truth, however, I have never really
looked upon the opposite of faith which is my
natural portion, even though it had often been
presented to me.

The above mentioned inborn poverty of spirit
(armuthseligkayt) undoubtedly corrects this false
faith. In actual fact I find all along that this
inborn sickness or poverty of spirit does not dimin-
ish; the more I spruce myself up, the more it is
bound to increase.

Compare this to an evil tree whose nature
does not become better but rather worse the more
one pampers and tends it. There can be no change
unless one gets to its roots and pulls them out
completely. If you would like to come into some
money, yet have none at all, you may claim to have
one thousand gold pieces as long as you please to
no avail. Since you have none at all, you should
not /21/ claim that you have any, lest you greatly
mislead people, fooling yourself most of all.

I earnestly wish that I had faith, that is,
life. Since it is not found in me by nature, I
can deceive neither myself nor others. Indeed, if
I said today that I have faith, I would likely
prove the contrary tomorrow; however, it is not I
but truth which I feel to some degree in my
inward being.

I know it for a fact to be the truth. Therefore, God willing, I shall give [truth] a hearing

for what it might say to me. I shall oppose everyone who wants to deprive me of it. Wherever I
shall find truth in a creature, be it lowly or
exalted, I will listen; to whatever place it may
point, I shall go; the things it drives me away
from, I shall flee.

When I seek to plumb the depth of Scripture
on my own, I do not understand a thing. But when
it [truth] drives me, I comprehend, not because of
merit but on account of grace. By nature I cannot
believe in Scripture. But that which is within
me--not my own, I say, but the force that drives me
on without the aid of my will and doing--drives me
to read Scripture for the sake of its witness.

Thus I read it and find testimonies that are
in part very strong in attesting Christ to be the
power that spurs me on. Scripture proclaims him
to be the Son of the Most High. For the reason
stated above, I dare not say that I have this
faith, even though I know that my unbelief cannot
endure in his presence. Therefore I say: "So be
it in the name of Almighty God whom I fear with
all my heart: 'Lord, I believe, help thou my
unbelief.'" [Mk.9:24] Thus with Peter, I regard
Scripture to be a lantern which shines in the
darkness [II Pt.1:19].

The darkness of my unbelief is in reality
great by nature. Scripture, the lantern, shines
in the darkness. By itself (it is written by
human hands, spoken with human mouth, seen with
human eyes and heard with human ears), it is unable

to remove the darkness completely.3 But when the
day breaks in our hearts, the eternal light, the
morning star, faith like a mustard seed, which
presently /22/ points to the sun of righteousness,
Christ (as Scripture also testifies of Jacob, the
Patriarch) [Gen.32:32], the darkness of unbelief
is overcome instantly. This has not yet taken place
within me.

Since such darkness is within me, it is impossible for me to understand Scripture fully. But
if I do not understand it, how can I draw faith
from it? It would mean to receive faith from itself,
if I take it before it has been offered to me by
God. Indeed, he who cannot await the revelation
from God, but undertakes the work himself which
properly belongs to God alone, surely makes a
laughing stock (einen wüsten Greuel) of the mystery
of God which is recorded in Scripture, and perverts
God's grace into wantonness (licentiousness) as is
recorded in St. Jude's Epistle [Jude 4] and in
II Pt.2:18.

For this reason very many sects and schisms
arose in days gone by, after the passing of the
Apostles. They were all armed with poorly understood Scripture. Why poorly understood? They
plunged into it in utter presumptuousness and
accepted a false faith before they aspired to the
right faith from God.

Therefore Peter[II Pt.1:20f.] states correctly
that Scripture is not given to one's own interpretation, but that it belongs to the Holy Spirit to

expound it correctly who has also given it in the
beginning. Every man must be certain of the interpretation of the Spirit beforehand. If this is not
the case the interpretation is false and worthless
and whatever is false and worthless can be disproved by other testimony of Scripture. This is
what I am doing for the love and honor of God. I
do not mean to offend any one or disparage anything,
except it be truly "nothing."

From the above you may partly see what I
understand by Scripture, sin, righteousness of
God, Law and Gospel. But to make my definition
brief, I shall speak of the latter four in the
following manner:

Unbelief alone is sin, which is destroyed by
the righteousness of God through the Law. As soon
as the Law has done its part, the Gospel takes
over. By the hearing of the Gospel comes faith.
Faith knows no sin and where there is no sin, the
righteousness of God dwells /23/.

It follows that the righteousness of God is
God himself. Sin is whatever rebels against God,
which in truth is "nothing."

Righteousness works through the Word which was
from the beginning. It is therefore divided in two,
namely the Law and the Gospel, because of the two
offices which Christ fulfills as king of righteousness. These are to destroy unbelievers and to
bring believers to life.

Of course, all believers at one time were
unbelievers. Those who have become believers had

to die first so that thereafter they would no
longer live to themselves, as unbelievers do, but
rather live for God in Christ. As Paul says, they
walk no longer on earth but in heaven Phil.3:20 .

David also testifies to this when he says that
God leads down to hell but leads also out of hell
[I Sam.2:6]. I believe all this to be true (may
the Lord break my unbelief); let him take heed who
attempts to overthrow or deny it. I am prepared to
write down later what I believe concerning Baptism
and the Lord's Supper. There is no time for it now.
The Lord be with us. Amen.

II.   On Baptism

I, John, Denck, further confess that I understand in truth (to the extent that truth has gripped
me) that all things which by nature are impure,
become even more useless, the more one tries to
wash them.

Who would undertake to wash off the redness of
bricks or the blackness of coal, whose very nature
is what it is? It would be wasted labor, indeed,
because their nature cannot be softened and
changed. By the same token, a man whose body and
soul are unclean is washed in vain outwardly, if
one does not begin to soften and change him
from within.

The almighty Word of God alone can descend
to and penetrate into the hardened abyss of man's
uncleanness as a driving rain can soften arid

ground /24/. Where this takes place, a struggle
begins in man before nature is willing to make way.
Despair grips him so that he thinks he will have to
perish in body and soul; he will not be able to
endure the work of God thus begun. Just as one
might assume, if a great flood came, the earth
would not endure, but would have to be washed away.
In such despair David cries out: "Lord God, help
me, for the waters have reached my soul." [Ps.69.2]
Such despair, be it great or small, lasts as long
as the elect is in this body and the work of Christ
begins with it.

     For this reason, not only John the Baptist
but the apostles also baptized in water. The
point was that whatever could not withstand the
water, could tolerate fire even less, which latter
is the baptism of Christ in the Spirit and the
consummation of His work.

     This water of baptism saves[I. Pt.3:21] not
because it removes the filth of the flesh but
rather because of the covenant of a good conscience
with God. This covenant means that whoever is
baptized into the death of Christ is baptized in
order that he might die to the old Adam as [Christ]
has died and that he may walk in a new life with
Christ as He [Christ] was raised. See Rom.6:4.

     Where this covenant is, the Spirit of Christ
reaches also and kindles the fire of love which
fully consumes whatever is left of our infirmities,
thus perfecting the work of Christ. After this
the Sabbath, the eternal rest of God, sets in. Of
this no tongue can adequately speak.

Where the outward baptism is administered in this covenant it is good. Where this is not the case, [baptism] is of no avail for the reasons given. Outward baptism is not essential to salvation. Thus St. Paul says that he had not been sent to baptize (which was not essential) but rather to preach the gospel (which was essential)[I Cor.1:17].

Inward baptism of which I have spoken above is essential. Thus it is written, "He who believes and is baptized, will be saved" [Mk.16:16].

On the Supper of Christ

I, John Denck, confess over again, as before, that I find myself unsound in body and soul, poisoned and truly full of fever. Whatever I eat therefore in this unsound, poisonous and feverish state of body and soul does not cure my illness, but rather heightens it. /25/ I also find that that which drives me on (not as I will but as it wills), as a faithful physician advises and instructs me that as long as the poison is in the blood there is no remedy for the fever until the blood is soothed and quieted.

This may be done in two ways, namely by abstaining from food or by bloodletting. To diet or abstain from food, means to refrain from strengthening oneself from within by inappropriate food, which is false comfort. Bloodletting means to accept outward suffering also, on the advice of the physician. All this is the work of Christ in the mortification of Adam. Now even though this

does not end as long as I am in the body, it begins,
nonetheless in the body and is partly suffered for
the sake of the covenant with God if I place my
will under the will of God in Christ the Mediator,
as was suggested above in connection with baptism.
Whoever is thus-minded and eats the living invisible
bread, will be strengthened and confirmed in the
right life.

Whoever is thus-minded and drinks the invisible
wine out of the invisible Cup, mixed by God from
the beginning of time through his Son, the Word,
will become drunk. He does not know anything
about himself any more, but becomes deified
(vergottet) through the love of God while God
becomes incarnate in him (vermenscht). This is
what is meant when we speak of the eating of the
body and the drinking of the blood of Christ
[John 6].

Indeed, the one who is thus-minded, as often
as he does what the Lord commands, i.e., as often as
he eats of the bread and drinks of the Cup, shall
recall and proclaim the death of the Lord [I Cor 11:26].
To him who eats and drinks physically also, it is
truly health and soundness of the body, because the
body has subjected itself to the Spirit and serves
him in truth: And that which is healthy and sound
cannot be anything other than the Word of God
which Paul often calls the sound teaching [II Tim
4:3, &c.] Since, however, it is invisible in the
visible bread and yet is nothing other than the
bread, it is consequently the invisible Word in
the visible body which is conceived from the Holy
Spirit, born of the Virgin Mary. /26/

Food and drink cannot be separated from each
other if they are to be of any benefit. Food without drink constipates and does not nourish. This
is what Paul means to say when he writes: "If I
had faith to remove mountains but lacked love, it
would be nothing" [I Cor.13:2]. Drinking without
food softens and intoxicates. Love without faith
cheats itself in its presumptuous claim that it
loves everything for God's sake. While this may
appear to be so for a while, it is nonetheless
untrue. Suddenly it breaks out for everyone to see
that love will love only that which love loved before,
even though that were evil, and that love always hates
that which speaks the truth to love, even is that were
good. Food and drink, if taken together, are useful,
indeed. Food comforts and strengthens; drink kindles
love and perfects that for which Christ came, which
is the washing away of sin, a task that has been
accomplished in the shedding of Christ's blood.

What has been said above of the visible bread,
can be said also of the cup. One can live without
this outward bread by the power of God wherever
His glory demands it, as did Moses on Mount Sinai
[Ex.34:28] and Christ in the desert [Mt.4:2]. Without the inward bread no one can live. For the
just one lives by faith [Hab.2:4; Rom.1:17]. He
who does not believe, does not live.

All this I confess with my whole heart in the
presence of the invisible God. To him I most humbly
submit myself on the basis of this confession. I
should say, not I; rather He Himself subjects me to
Himself, not to Him alone but to all creatures in Him.

I appeal to all creatures and to your wisdom, which is in the hand of God, by the name of the terrible and great God, that you judge me and my captive brethren whom I truly love, not according to appearances but according to the truth.

In this manner the Lord himself will judge when He comes in His glory on the day of the revelation of all mysteries. Amen. Amen.

I.2

CRITICAL EVALUATION OF
HANS DENCK'S CONFESSION BY
THE NUERNBERG PREACHERS
(1525)

<u>Schriften</u>, 3.Teil, pp. 136-142

Critical Evaluation (Gutachten) of Hans Denck's
Confession by the Nuernberg Preachers. 1525

Note:
     The evaluation here translated was made by
the preachers of Nuernberg whose chief spokesman
was the preacher A. Osiander. Denck and likeminded
radicals are shown to be heretical and therefore
dangerous to the uniform attempt at evangelical
reform to which the City Council subscribed. According to W.Fellmann the evaluation was likely written
between Jan. 16th and 20th, 1525.

     Worthy, honorable, wise, gracious, dear
gentlemen. You have summoned certain people during
the last few days who along with others of their
kind were to have been cross-examined by us the
preachers because of the errors of their faith
which they expressed and spread about freely and
unguardedly. However, a certain Hans Denck,
schoolmaster at St. Sebold School, proved to be
so skilled that we considered it to be useless to
argue with him orally. For this reason you ordered
him to answer certain articles in written form,
which he did. We have received these articles
from you, worthy gentlemen, and intend to answer
them herewith.

     First of all, he does not give straight-
forward answers to the articles which had been
given him by your excellencies for his justification. Rather, he attempts to elaborate and
color the thoughts and ideas of his mind (Scripture

never speaks as pointedly as he does), so that one
can perceive easily that another than the Spirit of
Christ drives him. ;The latter has spoken through
all the prophets and apostles in a manner quite
different from his. For this very reason his arguments should be suspect to every true Christian;
/137/ it is so plainly evident that his language
is not of the kind which the Holy Spirit uses
everywhere in Scripture, that we are almost certain that he [Denck] himself could not and would
not deny that.

Secondly, even if his confession had been
written by him in such manner and Christian understanding that one could accept his intent and
opinion, we nonetheless know of the wiles and the
evil of the devil, who in this manner seeks to
subdue and spoil the Word of God and its fruit;
for if one part speaks in accordance with Holy
Scripture, as the Holy Spirit is wont to do, while
the other part speaks according to its own ideas;
the two parts will inevitably clash in disagreement
and begin an argument in which each will attack
the other's truths (even though they be well-
intentioned), seeking to dismiss them. This,
indeed, would be Satan's pleasure by which love
is rent asunder and all fruit is despoiled. Just
as the tower of Babel could not be built directly
its builders became divided in language [Gen.11:1ff],
so we cannot accomplish anything with the Holy
Gospel, if we do not speak one language. This,
however, we must learn from Scripture by the Holy
Spirit so that thereafter everything will be understood more clearly.

Thirdly, he has been challenged to point out what he thinks of Holy Scripture. He might have done this briefly in the following manner: Holy Scripture is indisputably true in the sense which the Holy Spirit, who gave it, intended. In addition, Scripture speaks of Christ [John 5:39] and instructs us [Rom. 15:4f] that everything that has been written was written for our edification that we may learn patience through the patience and consolation of Scripture. See II Tim.3:16], "All Scripture, given by God, is useful for teaching, punishment, improvement, etc."

But he does not do any such thing; rather, he comes with cunning and discards Scripture as if it were of no use just because not everyone understands it. Yet it is clear enough. It does not take understanding but Spirit. Who does not know and understand what Christ means when He says, "Love your enemies, bless those who curse you, do good to those who hate you..." [Mt.5:44f]? We are deprived of the Spirit only if we have neither desire nor strength to do thus. In the same manner one may judge all Scripture. It is intelligible enough if one has first learned the language and knows the events to which it refers. Human malice, however, finding that there is neither desire nor love for that which Scripture says and teaches, invents its own meaning and interprets Scripture contrary to the Spirit of God /138/ in a manner of speech which suits its own conscience. Therefore Scripture is not to blame but rather human wickedness; consequently Scripture remains absolutely truthful and is further a tool for teaching, punishment, improvement and the upbuilding of faith as Paul says in Rom.10[:17], "Faith comes from what

is heard and what is heard comes by the preaching
of Christ."

It does not matter at all whether the prophets
or apostles have preached orally or in written form.
Scripture still is as prominent as preaching.
Faith comes by it and for the sake of this faith
the Holy Spirit is given [John 7:19]. For this
reason Paul says in II Cor.3:6 that they [prophets
and apostles] are "servants of the New Testament,
not of the letter but of the Spirit." This means
that believers receive the Holy Spirit by their
preaching and their writing. Thirdly, Scripture
is also a witness of Christ [Jn.5:39]. That he
[Denck] maintains that God alone gives faith and
anyone who derives it from Scripture has it from
himself and not from God, is a deception, typical
of this kind of prophet. It is indeed true that
God gives faith. However, He also gives it by
means of the hearing, as has been pointed out above.
The hearing comes from preaching or writing. God,
therefore remains the master and Scripture or
preaching the tool. As little as a master undertakes to perfect a tool, as little will God give
faith to those who belittle (despise) Scripture
or preaching. Note what the Lord says in Mt.10:14f,
"Wherever someone does not accept you or listen to
what you say, leave that house or town and shake
off the dust from your feet. Verily, verily, I
say to you it shall be more tolerable on the day
of judgment for the land of Sodom and Gomorrah
than for that town."

This Denck and his companions, however, do
neither care to listen to Scripture nor do they

know it except as testimony (as they freely confess
both in written form and orally). That is why
Denck has said for some time now that there is
something in him which offers resistance to his
malicious inclinations. However, he will not call
it by name, for he fears that he might be convinced
with the help of Scripture that he received the
same either through hearing or reading. To the
very end he insists that it is of Christ. Yet at
the same time he denies that he has any faith and
that he cannot glory in him, saying that unbelief
cannot withstand it (which he won't name). You
may well see from this where we stand with him.
If Christ is really within him who resists, drives
on, girds and leads him, he must have faith; if
there is no faith, however, Christ will have nothing
to do with him. If he insists on calling his faith
"no faith" until it is perfect (which can never be
in this life), he acts contrary to Christ and to
all Scripture. You can well see that it is a real
devil who thus stands against Christ, His word
and work.

     If Christ is in him, he must needs have faith.
If he does not believe, it is not Christ who spurs
him on, but the devil. If he insists that faith
should not be called such until it is perfect, he
acts contrary to Christ who taught differently.
You can see at once that an evil spirit works in
these people, who by such tricks as these attempt
to push Holy Scripture--an instrument by which God
effects faith within us--under the chair. That
indeed is his desire. For if we pay no heed to
the words of Scripture, Sodom and Gomorrah will
fare better than we [Mk.6:11].

In the fourth place, let him point out what
he says of sin. There he points out that he regards
unbelief alone to be sin. This is correct if he
only understood it correctly. That he does not
understand it though, will become apparent at once.

In the fifth place, let him point out how he
esteems the Law. He has given us a clue with these
words: Unbelief alone is sin. Sin is overcome by
the righteousness of God through the Law. Here is
his gravest error in which he surpasses not only
the Papists but the Jews also. For if unbelief
were sin then <u>faith</u> which comes through the hearing
of the Gospel and not the Law must cancel it out.
The Law does not cancel out sin. It only points up
sin and makes it apparent [Rom.3:20] ; it works not
faith but wrath [Rom.4:15] .

It is quite clear therefore that the Law
does not cancel out sin. Rather, it wakens sin and
makes it more forceful as Paul testifies in Rom.7:7-1?
when he says, "If it were not for the Law, I would
not recognize sin. I should not have known what
it is to covet, if the Law had not said, 'Thou shalt
not covet.' But sin finding opportunity in the
commandment, wrought all kinds of covetousness in
me. Apart from the Law, sin lies dead. I lived
apart from the Law, but when the Law came, sin was
revived. I died, however, and it came about that
the very Law that was given me unto life proved to
be my death. For sin finding an opportunity in the
Law deceived me and killed me by the same Law. The
Law is holy and the commandment is holy, just and
good. Did that which is good then bring death to

me? By no means. But sin, in order to show itself
as it really is, worked death in me through what
was good that sin might become sin of the highest
order through the Law."

      Thus Paul clearly testifies that sin is not
broken by the Law but merely quickened and made
strong so that it will kill us, as he acknowledges
in I Cor.15:56, "the strength of sin is the Law."

      If the Law could break sin we would not need
Christ. Everyone then who says that the Law breaks
sin, denies and dismisses Christ. Paul /140/ points
this out in Rom.8:3-4, saying, "For God did what
the Law (weakened by the flesh) could not do. He
sent his Son in the likeness of human flesh and for
sin. He condemned sin in the flesh in order that
the just requirement of the Law might be fulfilled
in us."

      Thus to condemn and break sin and to set
righteousness in its place, is a work of God through
Christ his Son, which could be accomplished by Him
alone and was unattainable by the Law. Thus one can
see the spirit of Denck who ascribes this power to
the Law (contrary to Scripture) in order that Christ
may be denied and pushed aside.

      In the sixth place, he must point out what he
thinks of the righteousness which is valid before
God. Here too he has answered correctly in saying
that the righteousness of God is God Himself. He
is wrong, however, in not ascribing to the righteousness of God, the power that casts out sin. He

credits the Law rather than faith with such power.
For he who believes in Christ, receives the Holy
Spirit [Jn.7:39]. The Holy Spirit and not the Law
redeems us from sin [Rom.8:2].

In the seventh place, let him point out what
he thinks of the Gospel. This he has not done
either. What could he say of the Gospel after all
since he has attributed everything that once belonged
to the Gospel to the Law? Nonetheless, he says
that the Gospel follows as soon as the Law has fulfilled its office. If the Law could indeed break
sin, what do we need the Gospel for? Truth is too
strong for people. They would love to oppose it,
but they cannot do so. He confesses that faith
comes from hearing and faith has no sin; wherever
there is faith there is no sin. In other words, it
is faith which breaks sin and not the Law. If
faith comes from hearing why then do they say that
they cannot receive faith from reading and preaching?
One may easily recognize Satan's evil intent here,
[Mutwillen].

In the eighth place, he must show us what he
thinks of Baptism. He says a great deal concerning
inward baptism and declares outward baptism utterly
useless, notwithstanding the fact that Christ himself has instituted it and ordered it to be practiced, as all the apostles have done. He does a
great deal of harm in this matter too.

For the inward baptism is the dying of the
old Adam, which no one can endure unless he be
assured by the Word of God that the very suffering

and dying of the old Adam is to his benefit,
ordered by God out of grace and not because of His
wrath. We find the same word and encouragement
with regard to outward baptism in Paul's words in
Rom.6:4, "By baptism we are incorporated into the
death of Christ that we may rise again as he rose."
He says further to the Ephesians [5:25-27] that
Christ has given himself /141/ for his Church to
sanctify her and he has cleansed her by the bath
in the Word that the Church might be presented
before him in splendor without spot or wrinkle.
You can see here that it is God's word alone that
cleanses, but the same is promised us in the bath
of baptism. No one may claim this promise for
himself therefore who has not been baptized. However, God's work remains unchained, for He can save
any man who desires baptism but cannot attain it
and receive him into covenant with Him.

        In the ninth place, he was to point out what
he thinks of the Sacrament of the Altar. He does
this with many words, not grounded in Holy Scripture, but invented in his own head. In addition,
one cannot make out what he means.   Does he mean
to say that it is only bread and wine? Why does
he say then that the invisible Word of God is in
the bread which is the visible body, born of Mary?
If he intends to say, however, that it is the body
and blood of Christ why does he say then that God's
Word is invisibly present in the bread if this
bread is merely ordinary bread?

        Now it is undoubtedly the flesh and blood of
Christ, even though the false gloss has gained
prominence which reads as if Christ had said, "My

body is the body given for you." This is a real
devil's trick. How then are we to explain Mark
[14:22] who says, "He took bread, broke it, gave
it to them and said, 'This is my body.'" He does
not go on to say, "Which is given for you." You
may see thereby that he speaks of that which he had
given them, "This is my body." More clearly, Paul
writes in I Cor.10:[16], "The cup of blessing which
we bless, is it not the communion of the body of
Christ?" Look at the physical Israel. Are those
who eat the sacrifice not in the communion of the
altar? In the same manner, we eat of the sacrifice which Christ has made, namely, His flesh and
blood and come into the fellowship of wine and
bread, which is the communion of the body and blood
of Christ. Look at the physical Israel. Are those
who eat the sacrifice not in the communion of
the altar?

        In the same manner in which Israel eats of
the sacrifice of the altar and is in the communion
of the altar, so we eat of the sacrifice which
Christ has made, namely his body and blood, and are
in the communion of the body and blood of Christ.
Therefore, let Denck explain his position, whether
he takes it to be wine and bread or the body and
blood of Christ.

        Finally, we shall make an effort to advise him
of his errors and to point to something better.
However, he indicates often enough that such is
to no great avail with him. For he states in his
writings that he knows his own position to be the
truth and that whoever undertakes to take it away

from him, will not succeed. /142/ Consequently,
he has circulated a copy of his tractate among the
congregation. He would not have done this so
readily had he intended to await instruction. For
should he have erred and be proven wrong, how can
he eradicate now what has been spread in the congregation as if it were right and without blemish?
You may further see how wrong these men are in
stating that they communicate with no one, teach no
one and intend to draw no one to their side while
they do not stop doing these things orally and in
written form.

Therefore, worthy, honorable and dear gentlemen, we have herewith not intended to answer his
statements but have written rather for your information. Otherwise we should have required more
words and time which would be in vain and totally
lost in any case. However, we desire nothing less
than that you continue to deal with him. It may
help in God's name. If it does not help, it will
be your duty, worthy gentlemen, for the sake of
divine order and your office to see that this
poisonous error (which they cannot leave off), be
not spread any further among the people.

Yours truly,
The Preachers of Nuernberg.

I.3

A SUBMISSION BY DENCK TO THE COUNCIL OF THE CITY OF AUGSBURG CONCERNING EVENTS AT NUERNBERG
(1526)

Schriften, 3.Teil, pp.132-133

A Submission by Denck to the Council of the City of
Augsburg Concerning Events at Nuernberg. 1526[1]

   Considerate, honorable and wise gentlemen.
I have been informed by the beloved young nobleman Bastian of Freyburg and by Jörg Regel that I
have been denounced to you, honorable gentlemen, as
if I had incited the town people of Nuernberg to
disobedience of the authorities and that for this
reason I have been expelled therefrom by the worthy
Council.

   I am not at all surprised to hear this about
me. Nonetheless, no one can truthfully establish
that this is indeed the case. Honorable gentlemen,
deign not to take offence at this my brief reply
which will be of harm to no one, not even to those
who accuse me thus. May God grant that their own
talk will be of no harm.

   Here is the story: I was a teacher there
[Nuernberg] for a year and a half. Afterwards I
got into an argument with Osiander (who was
preacher there) concerning certain words of the
Sacrament. Consequently, I was asked to appear
before the duly called Council to give account of
myself. Since Osiander could not corner me as he
had intended, he finally presented me with seven
articles and asked me to respond in writing, to
which he then would give his defense in a written
counterargument.

   The seven articles, presented to me are the
following: What I think of Scripture, sin, the

righteousness of God, the Law, the Gospel, Baptism
and the Lord's Supper.

Honorable gentlemen may you clearly perceive
therefrom that this had nothing to do with obedience or disobedience.

After I had presented my pamphlet, I was ordered
to leave the city eight days later without any
reply from Osiander. However, I am grateful to
God if it pleased Him thus.

Since I have settled here by your leave and
through the good offices of the young nobleman
Bastian of Freyburg and Joerg Regel and assumed
responsibility for a number of children in teaching
them Latin and Greek to the best of my ability,
and since perchance (it might happen by your gracious and kind permission) I might be given greater
responsibility still, I beg of you, honorable
gentlemen, not to lend a ready ear /133/ to idle
accusations against me which can never be substanti-
ated by sound proof.

It does not concern me at all if all the world
were to hear everything I have said and done as
well as everything which has been undertaken
against me. I should be only too glad to show you
everything, worthy gentlemen, if you so desire;
although I should rather point these out in the
presence of my opponents should there be any one
against me. I know well and have never objected

to submitting myself to human laws as long as
these were subject to the Law of God. For how
else could I accept judgment on the Last Day if I
am unwilling to suffer the judgment of the world?

   With this I humbly commend myself to you,
begging of you to permit me to carry on what I
have begun with your kind leave and hoping that I
can conduct myself in such a fashion that I will not
arouse your ill-will. In case I have done something
unwittingly or should do anything in future that
may displease you, honorable gentlemen, I humbly beg
your indulgence. I shall be found most obedient.
God preserve you, worthy gentlemen. Amen.

          Respectfully submissive to your Wisdom,

          Jn. Denck

II.4

THE LAW OF GOD
(1526)

Schriften, 2.Teil, pp.48-66

Note:
     The following pamphlet is generally accepted
as Denck's first major effort of his Anabaptist
period. His aim was obviously to appeal to a
readership inside as well as outside Anabaptist
circles. Not unlike Schwenckfeld and other Radicals
of the day, Denck attacked Luther's understanding
of the Law. He sought to challenge the Lutheran
doctrine of justification. According to Denck it
is deficient as evidenced by the fact that the
Reformer's preaching does not effectively get at
the moral and ethical problems of those who flock
to the new teaching.

     Denck's style in this tractate is not too even.
One has the impression, at times, of great haste
on his part or else of a certain awkwardness in
handling a highly complex theological issue.
Undoubtedly the author was cramming too many ideas
into any given sentence in his effort to counter
all opponents. The treatise Divine Order, by contrast, is eloquent and testifies to Denck's literary
craftsmanship.

     We have used Fellmann's text without incor-
porating variant readings except when these
seemed useful in understanding textual ambiguities.
For a reference to variant 16th century publications
one may consult Hans Denck Schriften, 1.Teil, pp.24ff.

The Law of God (1526)

How the law is abolished, yet must be fulfilled

Preface:

    No single age has been so evil that God did
not work something among men. For this no one
could ever fully thank Him. Yet again it has
never gone so well in this world that one had no
need to be concerned about some evil. I am not
saying that God in Himself is fickle or that He
rejoices in such turmoil. Rather, all flesh is
so perverse that even the best, which God gives,
is always misused. For this reason then God
always mingles the sweetness He gives to His
friends during their sojourn in this world with a
dash of salt that they may remain fresh and
neither rot nor become stale.

    Some there are (and they are in the majority)
who complain that the world is in an evil way
right now. This is so, indeed. Although the
world has always been an evil tree, it has never
borne as much evil fruit as in our day. /49/ One
can substantiate this from history books and chroni-
cles. But there is not that much to bewail as yet.
There is more, by far, to be thankful for unless,
of course, one looks askance at God. For (not to
speak of the hidden works of God) had he done
nothing but to arouse the whole world, causing
it to seek after truth and to concern itself over
error, what he has done cannot be compared with
all the treasures and honor of the world. He who
cannot thank God for these, shows clearly that he
loves worldly peace and quiet more than truth, and
that he cannot endure human fragmentation for the
sake of divine unity.

On the opposite side there are also a few who
rejoice that God has shown such grace toward men.
Their joy is not unfounded, for God cannot but be
gracious even when He is most angry. But as much
as one may rejoice, one should also fear; perhaps
even more. For at the time of reckoning (Heim-
suchung), those who are carefree and joyful will
be dealt with much more severely than those who
sorrow and expect nothing else. Therefore Scripture says also that it is better to go to the
house of wailing than to the house of revelling
(zechen) [Eccl.7:2]. He who rejoices in God to
the extent that he is willing to surrender to
Him and drink His Cup, can rejoice as long as he
pleases and he shall not experience failure. But
he who says he rejoices in the truth but does not
walk according to the precepts of truth would be
better off if he did not know the truth.

Unfortunately, the larger part of those who
rejoice, do so without improvement and of those
who wail, the majority do so without advantage.
One despises the other, thinking himself better.
Yet no one is a mite better than the other, as can
be observed from their fruits. The one group of
people claims to be able to locate God's will here
and there, yet desires neither to hear nor to
explore it. The others, by contrast, say and think
they know God's will fully, yet they do not do it
either. These claim to be able to walk in God's
ordinances, as they say, but they do not want to
so that they may thereby prove His laws to be of
little use. The others, on the other hand, say
they would gladly do God's will, but are not able

to. May God withhold His grace from them that they
might not justify themselves and blame God publicly.
For they do not want to be regarded as those of
whom the Lord says that He often tried to gather
them as a hen gathers her chickens, but they did
not want to [Mt.23:37].

   This is the evil and the corruption of which
unfortunately we have too much in the world at
the moment and which daily increases. All the
other evils, which one /50/ might name, such as
water, fire, sword, hunger and disease, are not
at all evil by comparison. Rather God appears to
be kind and father-like when confronting us with
such evils. Things would have turned out better
by far if the one kind of evil were not found
among His people. God the Lord our God, Himself
desires most sincerely that we might have a heart
to fear Him and keep His commandments [Deut.5:26].
Who is there, bold enough to want to or to dare
say that it is not His intention to give such a
heart? But He does not give it in any other
manner than as He has always done, namely, to the
hungry. Since now there are so few who are hungry
(however brash they may otherwise be), He tries
in every conceivable manner to arouse our hunger.
Blessed is the child who does not despise his
father's rod; he who despises it is not worthy
of the father's punishment. Truly, time passes
on; the careful one will have plenty to be concerned about; he who is sure and without worry,
let him watch what he depends on lest he find
himself naked at an inopportune time. Let every

one who can, make peace with his enemy on the road,
the sooner the better; Mt.5:25 woe to him who
waits for the judge to settle it. Dearly beloved,
do not begin any kind of quarrelling where there is
no need for it. Let each one suffer as much wrong
as he may be able to endure without harming him for
the kingdom of God; thus we will readily withstand
the wrath of God. I am greatly worried that we
sin grievously in uttering so many unnecessary

words on both sides. What value is there is shun-
ning all outward things at once? What value is there
on the other hand, were you to retain them all? If
you notice your brother treasures something which he
should not, teach him first to know God, then he
will treasure Him alone. If he does not do so, lose
few words over it. For if you destroy everything he
has and he heeds you, he will set another treasure
in its place which will be like the former or even
worse.   You, however, if you hear your brother say
something that is strange to you, do not refute it
right away, but listen first to determine whether it
is right for you to accept it, too.

     If you cannot accept it, do not judge him.
Even if you think him in error, be mindful lest
you be found in still greater error. Let no one
look to the mighty in this world, be it for their
strength, art or riches. He whose heart is set
toward heaven, let him turn it toward the despised
and lowly in this world whose Lord and aster is
Jesus Christ. He became the most despised among
men and was therefore exalted by God the Father
to rule over all creatures that can be named
or thought.

Woe to him who looks to any other goal but
this. He who thinks that he belongs to Christ,
must walk the path which Christ walked, in order
to reach the everlasting dwelling place of God
[Jn.8:51; 10:27f]. He who does not walk in this
path /51/, let him err eternally; he who points
to or walks on another path, "is a thief and mur-
derer"[Jn.10:1]. Such are all those who love God
and his Son for the sake of their own advantage;
this is the case with the entire world. God knows
who is not of this world, and he to whom God has
revealed this may rejoice that his name is inscribed
in the Book of Life.

Whenever I can convince someone of error and
point him to the right way, I delight in doing so.
To have this concern for him is not from myself;
rather, God has given it in my heart; He will also
grant that it may bear fruit. While I desire it,
I cannot coerce Him even though it were in my
power to do so. And should this my desire be in
vain, I shall be content, nonetheless.

Here is the reason for having written this
booklet on the Law of God. For I can see on both
sides that not only the people but also the shep-
herds go astray. He who does not go astray will
not need my instruction. But anyone who accuses
me of erring, he will have to prove me wrong, if
he can; thereby I shall know that he loves truth.
Should anyone convince me of an error but I still
refuse to recognize it how, when and where it is
appropriate, it will become apparent thereby who
has commissioned me to speak. If anyone has yet
another way of testing the spirit, I shall wait

for it in the name of God. I pray all those who
read this booklet for God's sake not to be hasty
in their judgment. Those, however, who would be
too rash, I implore by the future coming of Jesus
Christ to judge this as they desire to be judged
by the Lord. If they truly hope for the mercy of
God, I do rather like their righteousness; but if
they dread God's righteousness, I can rightly
challenge their claim of having obtained mercy.
If someone questions my being in the right, he does
not actually refute me. If my Lord tolerates
being thus blasphemed or obstructed, no one will
be able to save me but He alone in His own good
time which is the right time.

        I know well that some of my brethren consider
my writings subtle and strange. I don't even
bother asking them not to consider them thus. For
even the least wisdom which comes from God, is so
wise that the mind of the most learned cannot comprehend it, if they have not first become fools in
the eyes of the world. However, I do beg them as
I did earlier, not to despise my writings too
hastily and perhaps even consider them foolishness
ere they comprehend them and judge them on some
valid grounds. True wisdom can undoubtedly stand
on its own in the eyes of the world; a wisdom that
is not of God can and /52/ should be disproved on
the grounds of truth by a true friend of God. God
in heaven must surely regret that so much wisdom
must be employed, which would surely not be necessary at all, if the world were not so perverse.
Since we are so perverse, he also deals with us
in a perverse manner; God and all His host with Him

rejoice eternally if the world accepts such treatment. The man who deeply bemoans the evil state of the world will truly rejoice with God.

He whom the entire world confesses in words and denies by its deeds says, "I am not come to abolish the Law but to fulfil it" [Mt.5:17]. The carnal wisdom of this world, always passing off as the light of divine knowledge, tears these words out of context and says that Christ has fulfilled the Law, therefore we need not keep it, and if we too had to fulfil it, we would thereby imply that Christ has not fully done so. Thus these words are expounded for thus they serve our perverted nature to which everything that comes from God is pus and poison, as is witnessed by the lives of men.

If this insight were true, it would be irrelevant how one lives after one's conversion. The whole world is full of people whose fruits and lives were somewhat better before they gloried in their faith than afterwards. And these are supposedly the people by whose good works the heathen are to be moved to praise God the Father in heaven [Dt.4:6; Mt.5:16] Indeed, as are the works of these people, so the heathen exalt God. For they say to us with derision: "What sort of God do you have?" As if to say, that he is either not merciful (as you insist) to let you err thus, or else that he is not all-powerful and unable to help or punish you. Lord, Thou mighty God, do what Thou wilt not left undone, for Thy name's sake, that the perverse may abstain from what they ought not to do. Amen.

You say: Is it not true though that Christ
has fulfilled the Law? [Rom.12:4ff; Eph.4:1ff;
I Cor.12:4ff; Rom.8:1ff]. Answer: Not a single
law that has ever been conceived or written
is complete until it is perfected in the body of
Christ. Whoever desires to be a member of this
body does not realize the Law in exactly the same
measure as it is found in the head, must take care
lest he cheat himself. For whenever the members
do not concern themselves with what the head does,
something is not quite in order. /53/ A member
that does not share weal and woe, joy or sorrow
with the head, is surely a useless and dead member.
It is deprived of all the benefits of the body as
if it were not part of it [the body].

You say: "Has not the head made satisfaction
and fulfilled all that can be accomplished on
behalf of the members?" Answer: Indeed, he has
made satisfaction and has levelled the path which
no man could otherwise find that one may walk
therein and reach life [Jn.14:6]. Whoever does
not walk it, does not reach life; for him the
path is useless. He has fulfilled the Law, not
to place us above it, but to give us an example
to follow Him [Jn.13:15].

You say: "If He has done no more than pre-
pare a path whether or not anyone will walk on it,
He would be no greater than Moses. The path would
remain untravelled since we all are crooked and
lame." Answer: Although Moses was merely a servant in the house of God, the Son was not ashamed
of His office, which was to expound the Law. Moses
not only expounded the Law, but enabled men also

to keep it by virtue of the power of the Word which
had been laid in the hearts of the Jews [Dt.30:14].
However, Christ has accomplished as much more, as
the son in each household is superior to the
servant [Heb.3:3ff]. Christ has not only outwardly presented or written the Law for His own
[people], as did Moses, but He speaks and writes
inwardly in the heart from the creation of the
world to its consummation. He who has the Law in
his heart, lacks neither a path nor feet [to walk
with], light nor eyes [to see], nor anything else
that is essential for accomplishing the will of
God. Yet neither path nor feet are of any avail
to him who does not have it in his heart, however
well it may be with him otherwise. Let each man
take heed not to deny what he has, so that he may
not get what he would rather not have and be
deprived of that which he momentarily does not want.

You say: "No man is able to fulfil the Law."
Answer: Indeed, no ordinary man can do it.
Believers, however, can do all things [Mk.9:23],
not as men, but as those who are one with God and
are free of all creatureliness, even partially
free of themselves. It is impossible for men who
walk according to the flesh to do any good. Such
men should know that they are living in lies and
not in the truth. In actual fact all understanding,
will and the power of every creature is God's and
one with Him. Whoever desires to have a special
or another understanding, will or power against
God's will, may well imagine he has something
which in reality he does not have and /54/ may think
he lacks that of which all creation is full [Jer.23:24

Because of this one lie alone it is true that the
Holy Spirit testifies through His own that there
is something in men (be it understanding, will or
power or whatever) which is against God. Let him
who has understanding take care that he is in
truth not against God. Indeed, this very delusion
of which I speak is nothing. But he who is thus
deceived, does not fare any better for it. The
more he wants to be something he is not, the more
God, who in reality has never been against anything,
will be against him. Thus it happens that a thing
is impossible which actually is very simple. And
again that which was truly impossible (since it
does not exist) is nonetheless its very nature
and attribute. You say: "The apostles walked in
the Spirit. Nonetheless, they speak of customs
and ceremonies as of a burden, which neither they
nor the fathers have been able to bear [Acts 15:10].
How then can the highest commandments be easy?"
Answer: Ceremonies are an outward order, given for
 their improvement to the common people of Israel
to whom all spiritual language was foreign. Thereby
they were to be reminded of the simplicity of all
laws which had been revealed to Adam in paradise
from the beginning, namely to love God above and
to hate whatever may hinder love. For this is
the apple which God denied to Adam and all mankind
with him [Gen.2:17], namely, each and every
creature, toward whom man may develop love rather
than toward God. He who has this simplicity truly
in heart is free of and unencumbered by all ceremonies. Now where it would hasten the advancement
of said love in others, he must needs adhere to
ceremonies; where it would hinder, he must needs
refrain from them [cf. I Cor.9:20f].

It follows that the highest commandments of
love are not difficult to the apostles and to all
illumined men, as John says [I Jn.5:3]. The same
goes for ceremonies to the extent to which they
are productive of love as has been said. Wherever
they hinder higher worship, however, it is true
that they are an intolerable burden to all illumined
men. For this reason, therefore, all followers of
Christ are free of all ceremonies in order to make
room for improvement. He who does not truly follow
Christ, if he be a Jew, remains still under the
Law; if he be a heathen, he remains one still and
can neither glory in the Gospel nor in the Law.
Whoever fulfils the law of love, truly fulfils all
ceremonies also [Rom.13:8], even though he may
never give them a thought. He who takes in plenty
of ducats, would let all inferior change go by; in
fact he would find it difficult to handle the
latter, not because he despises it, but rather
because he would not want to miss out on the
higher currency. He who has plenty of ducats, has
money to spare even though he may not have a
farthing.

You say: He who has faith, fulfils God's
laws in spirit. Answer: Whoever fulfils God's
laws, loves His entire Law and likes to hear about
it. He who can't bear to hear the curse of the
Law, has actually /55/ not yet escaped it. But
the one who is under the curse is not in faith;
where there is no faith, there is no fulfilment.
One can detect the unbelief of all false Christians
who create their own laws and rootless faith
because of their dislike of hearing God's ordinances.

You say: No one lives without sin, therefore no one can keep the Law. "If we say we have no sin, we deceive ourselves and the truth is not in us," as John says[I Jn.1.8]. Answer: We are all fallen on account of sin. The less one acknowledges this, the more one sins: the more one bemoans it, the less does one sin. He who once has bemoaned it in truth, is born of God and sins no more. Everyone who sins, has neither seen nor known God. John and the truth affirm all this openly to him who has ears and eyes [I Jn.3:6].

You say: Why then does Paul say: "The good which I desire, I do not do and the evil which I do not will, I do?" [Rom.7:19]. Answer: Paul was a man under the Gospel as well as under the Law, but he was a new man. Consequently, he experienced as much, if not more temptation to sin after the new birth as before, but he did not sin. For no temptation is so intense with the elect that resistance and victory are not much stronger [Cf. I Cor. 10:13]. However holy one may be, he finds nothing wholesome in the flesh, i.e., he himself discovers that of his own accord all laws and ordinances of God would likely go beyond his strength. Therefore, he moans and wails after the flesh not because he has been overcome (for his Lord conquers within him also) [Rom.6:11], but because he would rather be free of the conflict. But according to the Spirit he rejoices and triumphs exceedingly, for there he perceives victory and salvation, greater than he can express. He is well pleased, however long may be the battle. Indeed, the more conflict in the flesh, the more peace with God. Thus after

long and extensive wails Paul can say with grateful
heart: "I thank God through Jesus Christ our Lord:"
[Rom.7:25]. What does he thank God for? He thanks
Him because He gives him much more than he could
ever ask.

        You say: He thanks God because He does not
count sin against him. For even though he sins,
it is not he who does it, but sin which dwells in
him [Rom.7:17]. Answer: Is it enough for one who
gets a divorce to excuse himself with such an
answer? One may indeed let such an answer get by,
but such a one would have no part in the kingdom
of God [Eph.5:5] and the law orders him stoned
[Cf. Lev.20:9ff; Dt.22]. He who cheats his brother
of a farthing does not love him. How would you
be able to give your life for your brother if you
begrudge him that little bit and take it from him?
How should one whom the world cannot rightly punish
be excused by God, who also justifies what the
world considers to be good? Let no one deceive
himself. He who does not love his brother, certainly does not love God either, /56/ for he does
not keep His commandments [Cf. I Jn.5:2]. He who
loves God, has his heart constantly with God, and
is sorry to say an idle word or do a vain deed,
not to speak of sin. Whoever seeks amusement in
idle words, proves that God bores him. But whoever
is sick of God, has never tasted how sweet He is.
A friend of God considers to be a sin the smallest
trifle, which he thinks, speaks or does without
God's prompting, as has been said. In similar
fashion Paul too has bemoaned sin yet had nothing
to do with the work of darkness [Eph.5:11] .

You say: Did not David in the Old Testament
and the Corinthian in the New, commit adultery
although they knew the Law [II Sam. 11; I Cor.5:9]?
Yet God has again received them, although they
had been outcast for a time. Answer: The entire
world is in sin unto death, but it is none the
better for it, for there is not one moment at
which God may not visit (heimsuchen) and recompense
the world according to its deserts. If then the
servant who does not know the will of his Lord, must
be wary of such wrath, how much more so he who
knows His will. Indeed, such a one is in the fangs
of death, he is dying and God does not owe him
anything better. He who is dead cannot ever live
of his own accord nor live his life over again
(whether God will give life to him, He alone knows
and is capable of doing). Therefore Scripture
says shockingly, he who tastes of what is to come
and falls from it, cannot return [Cf. Heb.6:4;
10:26; II Pt.2:20; Mt.12; Lk.11:24ff]. But,
there are unfortunately few men who have this
foretaste, as one may observe in life. He who has
it, follows it; he who recognizes the kingdom of
God in it, also allows it to rule. Woe to him who
knows God, yet remains a slave to the flesh. It is
true enough that God is merciful; one reads that
He has accepted many great sinners. Yet, however
merciful He is, one reads little, indeed, of those
who sinned after they knew the truth and have been
accepted again. These are set as an example for
us that we may fear His wrath and not underestimate
it; to extol His lovingkindness (mercy) and not
misuse it. He who truly fears God is safe from
His wrath, but to a transgresser (freveler) even
mercy serves unto damnation [Cf. Lk.1:67ff; Rom. 3:8].

You say: "The Lord says through the prophet that 'he will not recall his sin if a sinner repents' [Ez.18:23, 31; 33:11]; I hold to that." Answer: The Lord is trustworthy and merciful. More so than any man or angel could ever utter! But what kind of conversions takes place, one may see plainly every day; that is, people seem to get worse with time, or where there is improvement, it is merely for appearances. The tree may look good in all its foliage, but it bears nothing but crab apples. We show as much repentance from sin as one who slaps his brother's face and then says: "Forgive me, I did not mean to do it." Beloved brethren, there is a great deal to be desired. Conversion must be from the roots up if we are /57/ to come into the presence of God, lest a sinner turn into a hypocrite who surpasses all sinners.

He who desires to be a new man, but cannot leave the old life is like a pig which has just been washed and returns promptly to the mud puddle [II Pt.2:22]. Let him take heed where he stands with his plans who puts off conversion to some future date and relies on this. Reason: He who loves God does not intend to remove himself from Him; but he who has never been with Him, yet dearly longs to come to Him, is not to impose any limits on himself. For whoever postpones the good, indicates thereby that he does not need it greatly [Cf. Prov.24:12ff]. He who intends to buy the oil only when the bridegroom arrives, will miss the wedding [Mt.25:10].

You say: What good is it to repent? For if everyone has broken the Law once, no one will be

saved, according to what you say. Answer: If God
has made something once and someone breaks it,
God can nonetheless restore it. If he does not
want to restore it again, it is and remains broken
as before. A damage mended is no damage at all.
God the Lord of heaven and earth has established
a salvation by which satisfaction is made for any
damage [Rom.5:1]. The penance must be as hard on
the flesh as the breaking may have been easy; it
must be as much in keeping with the Spirit as the
other was against it. The amount of which God and
the Law had been robbed by the one must be restored
by the act of satisfaction [Cf. Eph.1:18f; Col.1:21f].
Blessed is the man who finds such work in himself
and gives way to it. He who does not desire it,
deserves nothing better than condemnation. If God
could give such a one anything better he would do
it gladly. Indeed, he would give it, if we could
but receive it; for no one can receive anything
from God unless he be prepared, when it pleases
God, to receive it against his own desires. He
who prays God for wisdom and cannot suffer God to
give him foolishness, does not ask that God's will
but rather that his own will be done. As long as
man will not surrender salvation out of his own
grasp, he will not achieve it. As long as he
fights condemnation, he cannot shake it off his
neck. Should a perverse man truly say: I will
gladly forfeit salvation because it is God's will
and willingly accept condemnation on account of
God, God would indeed show Himself none other than
good; He would have to give him the best and most
precious that He has, namely Himself.

You say: If satisfaction has to be made to
fulfill the Law, Christ is in vain. Merit is

upheld and grace rejected. Answer: No one can
fulfill the Law who does not know and love Christ
in truth. Whoever fulfills the Law through Him has
merit, but no glory before God [Cf. Lk.18:13f], for
all glory belongs to God by whose grace /58/ a way
is opened that had been closed to the world. Therefore merit does not properly belong to man, but to
Christ through Whom everything that man has is given
him by God. Whoever seeks glory in this merit, as
if he has achieved it himself, destroys grace
through Christ.

He who says, on the other hand, that one
need not keep the Law makes a liar of God who has
given it to be kept, as all Scripture testifies
[Dt.32:46]. This is what all those do who say
it [the Law] is not given to be fulfilled but only
that one may recognize oneself in it--as if it is
enough to know oneself to be evil whether one
remains evil or not. Moreover, the spirit of the
one who says he cannot keep it, is not of God,
for he does not confess that Jesus Christ is come
in the flesh [I Jn.4:3].

He says in his heart that Christ is 10000
miles from him. All those who do not know God
(this includes the entire world), pursue this line.
He who says he knows God, but also speaks like
this, is truly blind, for he does not want to see
the truth which he must see. It is a feeble lie
to insist that God's laws are impossible to keep
when Scripture expressly states that they are easy
and not difficult [Dt.30:18; I Jn.5:3].

Falsehood is recognized from the fact that one
cannot hear the truth, for falsehood cannot be

upheld over against it. He who accepts carnal
truth but intends to overlook spiritual truth is
one who does not place two contradictions in
Scripture on the same scales. Although he draws
on the two, he only gets a half truth. A half
truth is worse than a lie, for it is offered for
truth [Cf. Prov.24:21]. He who is a true student
of Christ, keeps the total Moses, even though he
might never have read him. He who does not keep
Moses and in addition does not even want to hear
him, hears God much less [Mt.25:38]. Whoever does
not wish to see him will on this account go blind,
for he (Moses) speaks not his own, but rather God's
word which can never be overlooked without conse-
quences. Indeed, everything that God has spoken
through Moses must be fulfilled in truth [Mt.5:17ff] .
/59/ It will be fulfilled as surely as if He had
spoken through Christ or the prophets; therefore
the belly of all carnal Christians will burst;
just as they fear.

    You say: Why then is it said and written
that the Law is set aside [Heb.7], that it is too
weak for justification and that the just man has
not been given any law? [Rom.8:3; I Tim.1:9; Rom.5] .
Answer: The one who has received God's new
covenant, i.e., in whose heart through the Holy
Spirit the Law was written, is truly just. Whoever
thinks he can keep the Law by following the good
Book ascribes to the dead letter what belongs to
the living spirit [Cf. II Cor.3:6]. He who does
not have the Spirit and presumes to find it in
Scripture, looks for light and finds darkness,
seeks life and finds utter death, not only in the

Old Testament but also in the New [Cf. Eph.1; Col. 1];
for this reason the most learned men are most
highly offended by the truth for they think that
their understanding (which they have so tenderly
and with great wisdom culled from Holy Scripture),
will not fail them. If now--to top it all--a car-
penter's son comes along, who has never gone to
school, and proves them to be liars, where will he
have learned it from? [Jn.7:15]. Therefore they
assumed that he rejected the Law, because he would
not accept their literalistic misunderstanding. My
brethren, such happens to this very day. Blessed
is he who is not offended by Christ. He who truly
possesses truth can determine it without Scripture.
The scribes could never attain to this because they
did not receive their truth from the truth but they
keep stealing it from the witnesses of truth [Jer.
23:30]. For those, on the other hand, who have it
in their hearts, as was said, the written Law has
been abolished [Cf. Eph.2:15; Col.2:14, 20]. Not
that they may discard it; rather, even though they
do not always understand its full testimony, they
have truth and righteousness in their hearts by
which they are not misled. Scripture amply testifies to this even though they do not recognize
it. But to the extent to which one does not yet
know God, love Him and keep His commandments, to
that same extent he must be subject to all laws
which convict him of wrong and punish him.

     The more these are held up to him, the more
hateful they become, for they are not capable of
straightening him out even though a prophet or
apostle may have written them; first of all, the

ground and root of evil must be revealed to him,
which is that one hates God whom he loves in his
heart. Only then does the power of the Most High
take effect in his heart without intermediaries for
God Himself is the true means, beginning and end
of every good. He [learns to] fear, know, love
and believe in God which /60/ no creature or crea
turely thing in heaven and on earth can ever give
him. Wherever this does not come about, no created
testimony can help, but will rather create hypocrisy
if it is cold [indifferent]; or, the better it is,
the more it leads to hatred of God; this is exactly
what Paul means when he says "the Law came in to
increase sin...." [Rom.5:20].

     You say: If this be true it were better that
there were no Law and that no one would preach it.
Answer: He who is not in God, but is to come to
God, has to recognize first of all that God is not
in him [Rom.7:7]. The more strongly and truthfully all creatures and creaturely things testify
against him, the more his enmity against God grows,
until it cannot grow greater, so that God alone
may receive all glory and not any creature, however
holy and good it may be. Not that God finds pleasure in such enmity. Rather that the flesh has no
other way to get rid of sin by itself except to get
tired of it. A witness who can prove to the world
and to all false Christians that all their deeds
(tun & lassen)--even the most sparkling--are darkness, is known by God who has sent him even though
he continuously stirs anger against God. For God
knows to what advantage this is. The one who tells
the world what it likes to hear and does not touch

the very heart of the false Christians is God's
uncalled and unwanted servant [Cf. Jer.23:9ff].
A true messenger of Christ can present his Master's
best message so that it appears ugly to all flesh
as long as flesh is unwilling to accept it in truth.
He who presents it in such a fashion that it becomes
pleasant to pigs and dogs is a workman who does not
esteem highly his Master's treasures and has no
intention to invest his talent if he can come out
without great damage. Only he who rightly proclaims
God's wrath, may also proclaim His grace fruitfully
[Cf. Ez.3:17ff; 33:1ff]. However, if he is silent
about the one or condenses it, he can neither speak
of the other nor proclaim it. However, where the
above-mentioned enmity against God is overcome in
a man's heart by the power of God, there the Law
and the Gospel are heard with well-attuned ears
[Cf. Ps.40:3,9]. There the prophecy spoken through
Jeremiah is fulfilled which says that one will no
longer have to say, know the Lord, for that is the
highest and best knowledge [Jer.31:33].

However fully such a one may know God, he
rejoices nonetheless in all testimonies which come
forth from a truthful heart and a good foundation,
be they ever so lowly; he rejoices in all admoni-
tions which are written and spoken in truth. He
devotes day and night to the Law of God whether
or not anyone witnesses thereto. Indeed, all
creatures are bound to testify of Him who dwells
in their hearts and who has created them for the
purpose of proclaiming His glory [Ps.1:2; 19:1ff].
Not that it be /61/ sought after, loved and
praised and that he then turn away from God with
hatred and cursing. For this reason such a one

cannot esteem Scripture higher than that which
he keeps of the things it teaches him which is to
love God with all one's heart [Mt.22:37]. He who
honors Scripture but lacks divine love must take
heed not to turn Scripture into an idol as do all
scribes who are not "learned" for the kingdom
of God.

    You say: Is it wrong for one who does not
know God to value Scripture highly since thereby
he may be led to knowledge?
Answer: If one were to give you a letter which
promised you great possessions, yet you do not
know the writer, how good and rich he is, whether
he is as you had hoped, it would be utter folly to
rely on the letter. Even if he is what the letter
indicates, you can, nonetheless, not rely on the
letter until you have discovered for yourself
whether this really is the case. If you find
that he is indeed good and rich, you will say,
"dear Sir, let me be your servant, I don't care for
your letter for I desire no other wages than to
be your servant and for you to be my master." To
him who is not in God's house the letter is of no
avail; but the one who is in God's house, knows
without the letter how good the Lord is. He who is
in God's house yet is not prepared to do without
the letter, implies thereby that he does not trust
the Lord without the letter; in other words, he
cherishes the letter more than the Lord even though
this is expressly prohibited in the letter at risk
of losing what is promised therein. For this
reason you should never reject the letter, however
faithfully you may serve the Lord, for it is established also as a testimony against you, if you

should some day undertake a wrong Cf. Dt.31;
Rev.22:18f . If you do not keep the letter, you
cannot use it as an assurance either.

   If God does not do more--every moment and
hour--than what is to be recognized by His letter
only, with regard to His power, goodness and justice,
He will remain unknown for a long time indeed.

   He who does not learn to know God through
God Himself, has never known Him. He who diligently seeks God and is not made aware by God, how
He has been with him ere he even sought Him, has
not yet found Him and is far from Him Jer.23:24 .
Oh, who will give me a voice that I may cry loud
enough for the whole world to hear me that God the
Lord, the Most High is in the uttermost abyss of
the earth waiting for those to be converted who
ought to be converted Cf. Ps.139:8; Job26:6 . O
Lord God, what goes on in this miserable perverse
world that no one can find Thee even though Thou
art so great; no one can hear Thee, even though Thou
speakest so clearly; no one can see Thee, even
though Thou art so close to everyone; and that
no one knows Thy name, although Thou makest Thyself
known to everyone? Praised art Thou, O Lord for
Thou art merciful and just and all the perverse
must be brought to shame for they flee Thee and
say that they cannot /62/ find Thee Cf. Jer.2; 32 .
They turn their backs on Thee and (then) say that
Thou dost not want to be seen [Is. 55:5]. They have
plugged their ears not hear Thy voice [Zech. 7:11].
For they say, these perverse men, that they will
have to die if they would hear Thy voice; yet one
is to come to life by it. They themselves have

sealed their hearts with the safety lock of an
unknown false god, yet they say that Thou dost
refuse to be known by them. The world does not
like to hear all this and proves it unmistakably
by its works. Therefore, the time will come, as
God the Lord has foretold it by His servants and
His Son, that those who seek Him will not be able
to find Him. However much they flee Him, they will
not escape Him [Cf. Ps.18:27].

For as you trust God in falsehood, He will
meet you in truth to prove thereby to all those
who fear Him that He is in truth and that you
cannot believe because of falsehood. Blessed is
the man who gladly suffers in the truth what he
sought to flee when in falsehood. Such a one will
find everything which appears difficult, unpleasant
and evil to the world, easy, pleasing and good.
On the other hand, only that which the world considers easy, pleasing and good will be difficult,
unpleasant and evil for him. The one who finds
the commandments of God difficult, does not love
God nor does he know how good He is. And again,
he who does not know God, cannot love Him; he who
does not love Him, does not keep His commandments
and does not have life. The covenant of God and
the yoke of His Son are not difficult [Cf. Mt.11:30]
to anyone except to him who has never borne it.
The more the elect works in God's vineyard, the
less tired does he get [Mt.11:30]; to him who is
in God even work is rest.

You say: since all laws have been directly
commanded by God, it follows that customs [Sitten]
must also be kept, even though there is no truth

which states that one ought thus to be bound by
outward things. Answer: There are three kinds of
law which Scripture calls commandments, customs,
and laws. Commandments are those that flow from
the love of God and neighbor [Cf. Mt.22:37-40]. To
overlook them is to incur sin. To this the con-
sciences of all reasonable people testify Rom.2 .
He who does not love God, sins continuously, whatever else he may do. But he increases his guilt
by the measure with which he transgresses God's
commandments. Customs are external ordinances,
geared to natural and daily habits of men by
which they are to be reminded of the things which
are divine and eternal [Col.2]. All customs are
sacraments or signs [Heb.10]. He who knows their
import, may decipher the signs easily. The sign
that is not meaningful is an offence and a mockery
before God. It must be rejected as if it had
never been commanded, as Jeremiah says [Jer.7].
Laws are judgments that are established between
brothers to protect the innocent and /63/ punish
the unjust.

To him who seeks the kingdom of God in truth,
all laws are acceptable [Cf. Mt.5]. In other words,
he can tolerate all laws between himself and his
neighbor. He ought not and will not seek one for
his own sake, even though he may suffer gross injustice; he will oppose no judge as long as he metes
out justice. He himself will not judge and punish
any more than is beneficial for the kingdom of
heaven [Mt.18:15ff]. All commandments, customs
and laws which are laid down in writing in either
the Old Testament or the New are abrogated for a
true student of Christ [I Tim.1:9]. In other

words, he has written upon his heart the one word,
which is that he loves God alone. He knows how to
govern his every deed by this, even though he may
have nothing written in front of him. Should there
be a portion which he cannot understand within the
context, he need not despise the witness of any
part of Scripture. Rather, he seeks in all dili-
gence, holding one over against the other [Cf. IIPt.
1:19]. But he does not accept it unless it be
expounded to him by the anointing of the Spirit
[I Jn.2:27].

He withholds judgment on whatever he does not
perceive, awaiting a revelation from God. For any
faith or judgment which is not opened through the
key of David cannot be received without the likeli-
hood of grave error. Even though it may not pass
as unbelief, it is often much worse since it presumes itself to be equal to true faith. He who
has God's love in such measure that nothing can
either stop him or further him in it, really has
no other law. Whatever may stop or further him,
is dictated by love, not only through what is
written, but also through that which is not written.
Whatever is written is designed to this end:
blessed is the man who can use it rightly.

Therefore all Scripture is given for admoni-
tion, instruction and comfort [Rom.15:4; I Cor.10:11].
As long as a man is perverse, he cannot use it for
what it has been given. Scripture and the Law are
in themselves holy and good [Rom.7:12]. However,
in a perverse heart all things are perverted.
Thus nothing can help such a one, but God alone
without any intermediary.

God shall not envy the one who seeks to reach
the intended goal by means of written laws. But
since that cannot be, he has set up a fiery sword
[Gen.3:24], i.e., a burning and dissecting word
[Heb.4:12] that points to the life of Jesus Christ
which tastes bitter to all human nature. Whoever
ventures forth with this sword /64/ shall eat of
the tree of life [Rev.2:7]; he who cannot accept
and tolerate it from God, finds all life he seeks
in creatures useless even though God may not forever
begrudge his having it.

He who has the right goal does not need such
aids; the more one needs numerous aids, the more
one lacks in the end. Whoever does not have this
aim, however, has neither aids nor beginning in
the truth, for the three are one [I Jn.5:7]; if one
does not have one of them, one has none of the
three. The one thing, above all others is the
love which God Himself is; whoever does not have
God, cannot be helped by any creatures even though
he were lord of them all. But he who has God, has
all creatures, even though none of them existed.

If the people of Israel had been imbued with
the true love of God, there would have been little
need of many commandments. Customs especially
would not have required extensive jurisdiction.
The people could have done well in God's name without all these outward things. Every heathen is
in the habit of washing himself after touching
a cadaver or something unclean. Likewise, they
are accustomed to isolate lepers and menstruating
women and not to eat blood, fat and the intestines
of animals. Likewise, the greater number of unclean

animals, forbidden by the Law is considered
unclean for eating by the rest of the world, even
though they have not heard God's commandments.
Why then did God give these commandments to His
people? If they were unable to keep the natural
order of the flesh, which everyone knows and
praises, how much less were they able to receive
from God spiritual and divine laws, which no one
cares to heed. Further, He intended to show that
all human order and decency is all right with Him
as long as it is not set against true love [Cf. I
Pt.2:2ff].

He who acts against love, cannot excuse himself either with divine or human law, for all laws
exist for the sake of love, and not vice versa.
Since they [laws] cannot give love, they should
not hinder it either. Love, on the other hand,
gives all laws, therefore love can receive them
again, each one at its appointed time.

However, to this day it is wholesome to
recall in all undertakings how much love is wanting.
Therefore, a man who has once been cleansed of the
filth of this world should not take a piece of
bread without thereby contemplating how much God
loves him and how much he ought to love God, to
wit that God in his own fashion breaks Himself
like bread for the sake of man and man in turn
ought to break bread to the glory of God; that God
renounces His divinity and that man in turn should
renounce his humanity so that the sacrifice be
perfect and that love may become one as it was in
Jesus Christ the first-born Son of God and as is
yet to happen in all the elect. To the extent then

to which a man is one with God, he is free of all
the laws of time and place and not bound by them.
But he cannot enjoy such freedom if he wishes to
be subject to all laws. /65/ For whoever is not
slave to all creatures for the sake of the will of
God, cannot inherit the kingdom of God through
His Son.

You say: Why would such a distinction not
have been explained to the Jews in the wilderness?
Or did God withhold it from Moses, or did Moses
withhold it from the people? Answer: God is not
ashamed of His works, but does them publicly in
the sight of all men [Cf. Amos 3:7], therefore
He is not forced to withhold what He has planned
for future ages. Thus He has had Noah proclaim
the Flood and Isaiah, Jeremiah and other prophets
the destruction of Israel and Judah, Christ and
all apostles the great day of the Lord, in order
that no one may be able to say that he has been
short-changed. Not only this, but He has also
revealed beforehand the greatest works of His
mercy; however, quite often these were revealed
either in hidden words or to a few people only
[Cf. Mt.13; Mk.4; Lk.8:4ff; Wisd.6:24]. Reason:
The flesh cannot understand what God speaks unless
it has been humbled first. O that all the world
might hear; no one would then take offense at
the fact that God will not leave His Word unspoken
for long.

Moses well knew through God that there was
to arise a prophet in Israel after him who was to
explain the Law to the people on a higher plane
and lead them out of Egypt in another fashion than

he had done. But he could not easily reveal such
[knowledge] to the people with any great success.
For if the carnal people had realized that the Law
was to be expounded on yet a higher level, they
would have relied on this and would at least have
despised the customs (as some did, in any case) not
for the sake of truth but because of their own
interests [Cf. Lev.10; Num.16]. Therefore he
commanded the Law to be kept forever, even though
it was not to remain forever in that form as they
had thought [Cf. Dt.29:28]. They should have
known this from the fact that He told them that
God would call out a prophet like him from among
them, whom they were to hear [Dt.18:15]. If he
was to be like him he had to be equal to him in
working wonders and in the power of God; a thing
that had never been granted to a prophet, as
Scripture testifies [Dt.34.10]. The fact that
they were to hear him was an indication that his
speech would appear to be over against Moses, yet
in reality not against him. For this reason he
had set up a test case by which a true prophet
was to be recognized [Dt.13:2ff; 18:15ff]: namely,
that he would not lead to foreign gods but to the
One God of Israel, however strange his message may
otherwise appear; for all who point to the only
One God have only one truth and one message, even
though they may appear to be at some distance from
one another. Those, on the other hand, who do
not know how to unite with one another, may well
be false prophets, for /66/ they cannot be God's
servants as well. The one whom God has sent,
knows Him and His word is the Word of God. He
therefore knows how to judge [the Word] and to
harmonize it with the writings of all the prophets

and apostles. He who utters one single word which
does not agree with the truth, must be saying
everything, even if it be true, without the truth.
For he who has the truth has a well which can
never be exhausted [Is.58:11; Prov.18:4]. He has
no need to speak of the dreams and machinations of
his heart. Woe to him who does not take time
enough to draw water from the well.

     This is the goal which must be reached if the
Law is to be annulled--which was always far from
realized for all carnal Jews and Christians, even
though it is everywhere. For this very reason it
is not fitting for those under Moses to hear a
lot about the Law changing or to boast of the
present laws, since they have never really received
the Law. To the extent to which one has the Law,
its written statutes are abrogated. To the extent
to which one lacks the Law, one is subjected to
it. This insight, truth has prompted me to write
down and no falsehood can do anything to overcome
it. He who is born of God is bound to witness to
the truth. The one who despises truth will be
despised by God also. Cursed is he who does not
truly love God and keep His commandments. Cursed
is he who transgresses the least of God's commandments with an arrogant hand. Yet to the one who
cannot say "Amen" to this, God will, nonetheless,
reveal truth through His works. Blessed the man
who can say it (Amen) in truth; who will gladly
suffer the curses of the Law with all his heart so
that God's will alone be done; that He alone may
rule; that His name alone be hallowed and our will
be broken and the power of sin destroyed, and all
false praise be exposed now and forever. Amen.
This can, must and shall come about.

II.5

H. Denck

DIVINE ORDER
(1527)

Schriften, 2.Teil, pp.87-103

Note:
      Capito, one of the Reformers of Strassburg,
suggests in a letter to Zwingli dated 18 August
1527 CR 9, 1925, No. 643 that freedom of will,
the conversion and justification of sinners were
the topics of debate between Denck and the Strassburg preachers. On this evidence it has often been
held that the _Divine Order_ must have been in print
before 1527. However, since the ideas contained
in this document are found in Denck's first theological treatise, _Was geredt sei_ (Cf. LCC 25,
pp.88ff), it is not necessary to conjecture in
this fashion.

      Denck shows affinity here as well as in _Was
geredt sei_ to the thought world of Th. Muenzer
(cf. _The Prague Manifesto_). The author's style is
forceful and polished. He addresses himself to
the elect as a "servant of Jesus Christ" whose
task it is to delineate clearly the deceptive
words of scribes and hypocrites in order to prevent
his fellow servants from falling from their loftier
plane. The document has twelve short chapters in
addition to a Preface and a brief Conclusion.

      One need not subscribe to Denck's spiritual-
ism which contains traces also of the mystics of
the Middle Ages, to be impressed by the lucidity of
his argument and by the skill with which he clearly
shows himself "learned in the school of Christ."

DIVINE ORDER (1527)

God's order and the work of his creatures:
to destroy the fabricated, deceptive excuses

of the false and corrupt elect,[1] so that
truth may be enabled to accomplish the
eternal unchanging will of God.
    [Col.1; Eph.1]

        by Hans Denck

    To all readers and listeners I say with
Christ, in John 7: "He who desires to do the will
of God, i.e., (he) who dies to sin, must needs be
able to recognize the teaching which is of God."
For it is impossible that a false spirit deceive
him. [Jn.7:17, Mt.7:15ff, Mk.3:23ff., Eph.6:10ff,
I Pt.2:7ff; 4:4, I Jn.2:18ff; 5:4; Heb.10:23;
Rom.2:15; 5:3f].

    To the fellow citizens of the lamb John says
in I Jn.2:27: "The anointing which you received
from the Holy Spirit remains in you. You really
require no one to teach you since whatever you
learn by being anointed is true and not a lie."

    To the scribes Jesus says in John 5:39f:
"Search the Scriptures for you think therein to
have life; the same testifies of me, but you do
not want to come to me and live."

    To those who do not know God, yet bemoan the
vanity of all creatures [Rom.8:17ff; Dt.30:11ff]
I say, along with Moses and Paul: "Vanity and evil
you do see well, but the good, after which you
secretly long, is not too far from you, not too
high or difficult that you may not attain to it;
rather, it is in your heart and mouth. You cannot
altogether be rid of it even though it is against

your nature. If you oppose it, it does not bid
you do anything; if you want to follow it, you will
be wondrously led by it to the place which you now
despair of ever reaching."

I, Hans Denck, a servant of Jesus Christ, pray
endurance for all the elect who seek God in the
depth of their hearts and the ability to know His
almighty power, judgment and wondrous deeds in the
fear of the Lord. Amen.

        Dearly beloved, since you find within you the
beginning of the work of the eternal invincible
God, which has almost imprisoned your heart and is
intent on driving you away from the self-seeking of
carnal life (which you yourselves confess to be
vain and unsettled), give heed therefore not to
cast it into the wind nor to let it pass over your
heads [Ps.7:17, Ecclus.27:28], lest you be blown
away like chaff [Ps.1:4]. You treat this little
talent like a major possession. However, if you
do not invest it properly, no excuse will help you
very much [Mt.25:14ff]. Do you know that He who
has entrusted you with this talent, acts mightily
and expects to make a profit Himself? Since you
fear Him, why not wait on Him [Ps.115:9ff]? You
may say what you will, /89/ but you know full well
that the more you flee Him, the harder it is on
you [Ps.139:7ff]. Why do you bury your talent?
[Mt.25:25].

        If you say, we are unable to do anything with
it, you do not speak the truth. For no talent is
so small that it is not good for something [Mt.13:31f
but you do not want to do anything with it [Mt.23:37]

What causes this? You tire of the effort, slothful
servants that you are. You fear for your backs
 John 16:1 . Yet, you know how to indulge in food
and drink and in all desires. Who taught you that?
You say that you cannot help doing so since you
have been commanded to do so. Brothers, brothers!
How you malign the Most High, for you know full
well that He orders the very opposite, namely, to
do good; yet, you say He forces you to do evil
[Ecclus.15:11]. Your own will forces you [Jn.8:44],
but you seek to put the blame on God [Rom.9:19].

     You say it is written: "Those whom he foreknew,
he also destined to salvation and no others."
[Rom.8:29]. Look well unto these words, my dearest
friend, that you may not abuse them to your own
condemnation [II Pt.3:16]. For even though the
words of God are in themselves clearness and light
[Ps.19:8f], our darkness still does not comprehend
them [Jn.1:5], as long as we seek ourselves [Mt.10:
26f]. For this reason, Peter faithfully admonishes
us not to be too hasty with Paul's letters. But
it serves us right since we seek to draw the words
of God out of books and bring them across the sea,
but we deny them in our hearts even though Scripture itself (which we accept like liars and
thieves [Jn.10:5, 8, 10; Jer.23:1f; Is.22:11f;
Rev.1:3], gives testimony of how wrong this is
[Rev.3:2; Deut.30:11ff; Rom.10:5ff].

     Therefore we shall at this point briefly
contrast the order of God and the work of creatures ever since the beginning of creation, so
that we may show by the differences, how far those
men fall who, without God's express command, open

their mouths [Ps.50:16ff] to speak of the covenant
and mystery of God which they have never understood
[I Cor.13]. They teach the right path to salvation which they have never really walked on and
are not now willing to walk on [Phil.3:18f]. They
say that they have faith; as they believe, so they
say. They have not abandoned the old and have not
accepted anything new--as might be expected of
scribes and Pharisees. Brothers, he who has ears,
let him hear; he who suffers want, let him ask
God in truth and humility and He shall provide
[James 1:5]. Amen. /90/

Of the foreknowledge and ordinance of God and of
His unfailing mercy.

CHAPTER I:

        We know that God is truly good; if He were
not good (far be that from Him!), He would not
be God. Since He is good He has made and created
all things to be good [Gen.1:27]. Inasmuch as
man is evil, he is apart from God [Ps.10:3f, 11;
Eph.2:2] and His own nature [Jn.8:44]. Even
though man has of his own account, thrust himself
into death, there was death which God has not made
[Wisd.1:13], God remains nonetheless what He is
[Exod.3:7], that is, good. For this reason He
allows His sun to shine on the good and the
wicked [Mt.5:45]. He gives everyone the chance,
grace and strength to be converted [Mt.19:26;
II Pt.3:9; Is.33:11; Wisd.11:23, 12:10]. He causes
no one to sin [Ecclus.15:21]. The light which is
the invisible Word of God shines into the hearts
of all men who are born into the world. For God
has been in the world from the beginning and He

gives everyone who will accept it free choice to
become a child of God and to inherit the kingdom
of the Father [Jn.1:12] .

   To him who does not wish it, however, the
light shines unto judgment and damnation [Jn.3:18;
9:39] since He who desires willing service [II Cor.
9:7; Ecclus.35:10,20] would not deem it right to
force anyone against his will to render Him service;
likewise, He forces no one to do evil [Ecclus.15:21] .
God desires everyone to be saved [I Tim.2:4; 4:10;
II Pt.3:9], but knows full well that many condemn
themselves [Rom.9]. If then His will were to force
anyone through a mere order, He could say the word
this instant and it would happen [Mt.8:8; Lk.7:7],
but this would curtail His righteousness. If on
the other hand, His knowledge alone were to exert
force, He would will contrary to His own will and
mercy; this too is far from Him.

   Why then did God hate Esau before he was even
born, yes, before he could have done any evil
[Rom.9:13]? He Himself answers, [Is.48:8] "I know
that you would transgress, therefore I have called
you evil from your mother's womb."

   Why did he love Jacob? The answer of the
Lord, [Jer.1:5] "Before I had formed you in your
mother's womb, I knew you; therefore I con- /91/
secrated you before you were born." He knew well
beforehand that Jacob would not sin, even though
he might well have sinned [Ecclus.31:10] ; on
this account He loved him.

   To the extent to which Esau's sin and that of
all perverted men has been known by God from the

very beginning, their punishment and death has been meted out also, for God punishes no one undeservedly [Gen.8:21].

To the extent to which Jacob's righteousness and that of all the elect have been known by God from the beginning, their reward, the kingdom and eternal life has been prepared too [Mt.25:34; Jn.14:3]. But no one will be crowned, unless he first fight [II Tim.2].

Two paths of men--one leading to life, the other to death--Mt.7

CHAPTER II

There is a struggle when a man seeks to lose himself and does so by the obedience of faith so that he may overcome the evil which is in him [Rom.7; I Cor.9]. As a reward he attains to the true knowledge of God and of his anointed one [Jn.15:3f; 17:3]. Subsequently a friend of God knows that everything which he conquered he did not achieve by himself, with his own bow and sword, but through God, in the power of the Spirit of God [Ps.44:7f]. He is at peace with God [Ps.4:8] and stands grounded upon the firm rock [Mt.7:24]; no enemy can reach him; no spirit can lead him astray from the peace of the Spirit of God to which he has been ordained [Jn.10:5]. In such peace he is not aware of any unrest; death and life are alike to him [Phil.1:21; Gal.6:14]. He no longer cares for himself, but together with his king he is concerned with how to bring others to him, where he is [Rom.1:14; Jn.17:20]. Sin is

disobedience and unbelief [Jn.16:9]; it is man
seeking himself. Then his righteousness suffers,
because a man would rather let it fall to the
ground and be destroyed than suffer any damage
himself, if he can help it in any way [Mt.23:37] .

The penalty thereof is a hardening in unbelief [Rom.9:18] when man has set himself free to
do evil [Ps.1:4ff]: he now hates everything that
is good and finds pleasure and delight in everything which is wrong. Yet the godless one says:
"Why has God created me evil? I can't help it.
I too would be saved like everyone else; /92/ if
He intends to save me, He could well do it [Is.45:22;
Rom.9:15f] .

Then he makes a pact with hell [Is.28:15];
when he finds a just person, he will hate such a
one all the more ardently the closer he is to God.

Finally he says that everything pertaining to
eternal life and damnation is a lie and fanciful
invention; we live on until we die and then it is
finished [Wisd.2:1].

Concerning Hell, which is overcome by God or A
Change At the Right Hand of God [Ps.77:11]

CHAPTER III

The moment the godless man speaks thus, he
is in the place for which he has been destined,
which is hell [Prov.9:18; Ps. 115:17]. But he
does not necessarily have to remain there [Ps.77:16];

for even hell is open to the Lord and damnation
has no hiding place [Job 26:6].

Hell is not mightier than His strong arm,
except in the form of highest righteousness which
we call wrath, wherewith   He lays upon us the
pains of hell [Ps.18:6f]. He makes us aware of
our own misery so that we may call upon Him in our
despair and He may help us [Hosea 9:9]. This is
what Paul says in Romans 11:32, "God has placed
them all in unbelief so that he may have mercy on
all." Such work is accomplished by the word of
God which addresses men in damnation, saying, "You
have inflicted this upon yourselves. Do not therefore blame someone else. You deserve to suffer
what you yourselves have willed." As soon as a
man becomes aware of the Word, he is in part free
either to continue in his wickedness or to offer
up himself through suffering [Jn.8:36]. The more
one objects to suffering the more he condemns himself until finally he is lost in death. The more
readily one surrenders, humbling himself before
the power of God [I Pt.5:6], the better can the
Lord accomplish His work. Man then thinks that he
must go to pieces when it stirs within him. He
becomes empty and hungry and dissatisfied Amos
8:11f . From a distance he looks to the bosom of
Abraham [Lk.16:23]. He knows full well that he
deserves everything he has gotten, but he does not
yet know that God is close to him [Jer.23:24] and
that He still has mercy over all flesh [Ecclus.
18:12]. Moreover, Abraham and his own conscience
--/93/ indeed the Spirit of God Himself--appealing
to his conscience--speak of nothing other than
righteousness, as if the righteousness of God is
none other than almighty and merciful.

The Eight Beatitudes, Mt.5:3ff

CHAPTER IV

Eternal salvation begins ere we are even
aware of it when the Lord places us in the remotest
part of hell so that we become poor in spirit
[Mt.5:3], thinking that we are going to die within
ourselves. Unspeakable moaning and crying sets
in, for it appears God has utterly forgotten us
and has turned His back on us [Jer.18:7] as if
unwilling either to accept or to hear our crying
and imploring [Ps.22:3]. Yet just then the dawn
breaks forth [Gen.32:26] which is the comfort of
God's mercy; it is like rain at a time when the
earth is dried up [Ecclus.35:26]. Then the elect
say with joy in all meekness and patience: "Now
I know, Lord, that Thou dealest exceedingly well
with me in all tribulation and temptation. 'Thy
rod and staff have comforted me' [Ps.23:4]." Had
I known it before, even one thousand times as
great a temptation would not have affected me too
much." In other words, he delights in the righteousness of God and desires to unite with it so eagerly
that he forgets all his enemies in the process and
is prepared to forgive everyone who has harmed
him. His heart and soul are fully cleansed when
he forgives not only the creatures but also those
who have deprived him in the eyes of men. Then
this Israel, which means God's "warrior," is able
to see God freely, eye to eye [Gen.32:29f] as the
day breaks brightly and the sun shines. He sees,
I say, the one God, wholly and truly as He is.
What is written in Psalm 85:11 is then fulfilled:

"Grace and love have met: righteousness and peace
have kissed each other."

     God is gracious from the beginning. This we
know with certainty only after we have gone through
tribulation. But as soon as such knowledge and
trust spring forth from our soil, i.e., from
earthly man, by the power of God, righteousness
looks down from heaven. We see then that it is
not we but the Spirit of God who dwells and works
in us, returning to the Father that of which we
have deprived Him by robbing Him. Then /94/ peace
comes immediately so that the friend of God does
not even bother with it for himself. Rather, he
desires to help others to peace who are receptive
to it and for whose sake there has been created a
new inward unrest. But this does not really
appear as unrest to him but rather as an urgent
desire to show his love in its highest expression
to the brethren [Jn.15:13; Gen.3:15]. The elect
is then no longer an unprofitable servant [Lk.17:10]
who does only that which his master has hired him
to do, but he is a faithful servant and a friend
of his master [Mt.25:21] who does exceedingly more
than what the letter of the Law requires of him.
He seeks to serve his master even to his own hurt.
This is not required by the Law. He obeys not of
his own account. Rather, he has learned to do so
from his leader Jesus of Nazareth so that the Word
born of the Father from eternity which has wrought
in the same Jesus grace amidst highest disgrace
may also work in him according to the measure of
his faith [Rom.12:3].

God's <u>Will</u> <u>and</u> <u>Man's</u> <u>Will</u> <u>Separated</u>

CHAPTER V

There are essentially two, God and man.
Since they are two, each does his own thing,
good and evil, according to his kind [Is.55:8].
Not that God is a cause of sin, as the spirit of
the devil imputes. Rather, He causes the punishment which is contrary to our nature and appears
evil to us [Is.45:7; Amos 3:6]. Nor does man do
what is truly good [Gal.6:4; Is.46:12], since God
alone is good. But man seeks after truth and the
good which is in truth. The more a man sins,
the more he is separated from God [Is.59:1ff;
Lk.16:13]. If he is to become one with God, he
must endure what God from the beginning intended
to work in him, as he did before when God had to
suffer in him according to his nature [Is.1:2f;
Rom.9:14]. God in Himself neither works nor
suffers [James 1:17]; what He does create and
suffer He does through the Word, which since the
beginning is born of Him and has flowed forth
from Him through His Spirit. This Word does not
cease to work as long as there is a time or place
for it [Lk.1:68ff; Dan.7:16].

Thus God suffered with the people of Noah's
day the sin of the evil world up until the flood
[Gen.6:3], but He began to work His righteousness
in those in whom He had previously tolerated sin
up to the time of the death of Jesus Christ. The
latter became one with God and His Word through
His suffering [Lk.24:26; Acts 17:30f; Ps.18:36]
/95/ and descended into hell to preach to the

selfsame unbelieving spirits [I Pt.3:19f] that He
may perfect the work begun in those who believed
[I Pt.4:6]. Yet indeed, the Lamb which suffered
in Christ has suffered from the beginning of the
world [Rev.13:8] and shall suffer to the end of
the world [Mt.25:35ff]. The very lion of the
tribe of Judah [Gen.49:10] who has overcome in
Christ [Rev.5:5], has from the very beginning
overcome in all the elect [Num.23:19; 24:17] and
shall do so until the last enemy is routed [Is.30:
15; I Cor.15:26]. The lamb and the lion are the
one Word of God which is in all the world [Jer.23:
24; Wisd.1:7]. It is in our very hearts [Deut.30:
14; Rom.10:8], not idle, but to do the will of
the Father [Jn.4:34]. As long as we seek ourselves and disregard it, it suffers in us, unto
our damnation [Jn.3:19], as was said above, This
is the effect of the Word in us, even though we
do not know it [Jn.9].

The Union of the Will of God and Man

CHAPTER VI

When we are deepest in damnation we allow
ourselves and everything that relates to us to
be torn asunder with unspeakable pain [Job 7:20].
This is like a pregnant woman who at the time of
her birth has to accept her suffering. Indeed,
she does so willingly even though she cannot
yet rejoice in her offspring until she sees it
alive [Jn.16:21]. This is the eye of the needle
through which the uncouth camels have to pass, yet
cannot [Mt.19:24]. Indeed, we cannot do it ourselves but must suffer God to do it for us [Phil.

4:13].   To Him nothing is impossible [Lk.1:37].
As long as any of the elect vaunt themselves to
be something without the knowledge and love of God
[Gal.6:3; I Cor.13:1], He drives and tests them
until they submit to being nothing and the false
nothing is consumed [I Cor.3:7].   At that point the
eye of the needle, the narrow gate to life, becomes
wide enough; the yoke of Christ (which to the
world appears bitter and unbearable), becomes to
them wonderfully useful and easy [Mt.11:30].

     The more a man resists this consuming fire,
the more unrest it causes him [Job 9:29].   Christ
is of no use to him then [Jn.3:18], even though
He suffered for all [I Jn.2:2].   The more he
gives up his own, the sooner /96/ God is able to
reach His goal [Wisd.6:12ff].   The fall of Adam
does not hurt him, even though it has affected him
too [Jer.31:31ff; E z.18:21ff].

Man's Free Will And His Captive Will

CHAPTER VII

The closer to and more like his created origin
a man is, the freer he is.   The closer he is to
damnation, the more he is enslaved [Mt.5:20;
18:8].   However free he may be, he cannot do the
good except by suffering [Phil.2:13]; and even
though he may be enslaved, he is nonetheless free
to suffer what the Word brings about in him [Mt.
23:8f].

     He who says that he has no grace from God to
become pious is a liar, as are all men [Ps.116:11].

In fact, he even lies against God who pours out His
mercy upon all men [Ps.119:77; 145:15f; Ez.18:21;
33:11; Wisd.11:23ff; Ecclus.1,13,19; 18:4; I Tim.
2:4; II Pt.3:9; Mt.18:14], but He pours out his
wrath as well and even more plentifully [Rom.5:12ff;
Ex.20:6]; otherwise the godless would be without
guilt as they claim to be. But they cannot support
their claim [Jn.9:41; Rom.3:11f; Ps.57]. The perverse man who seeks himself (but does not want to
lose himself), will not find himself in all eternity [Ps.1:4; Mt.10]; he wishes to achieve something
and overcome before he has suffered; he wants to
believe before he knows what faith is; he wants to
be saved, but knows of no damnation; he seeks life,
but does not know death.

It is here that the two contradicting views
arise with some saying that they have free will.
Yet they do not even do an iota of that which
pleases God. Some say that they have no free will
because they see in part that they cannot do anything right. Yet they would freely suffer the
work which is done by the Word [Mt.23:4, 23].

As was said above, both these statements in
themselves are right. But they are both lies,
since men make them for no other reason than either
to boast of their freedom or else to talk themselves out of responsibility and to excuse themselves by saying "May God give as He can vindicate
Himself."

The first claim regarding free will is plain
boasting and foolish security which allows no room
for the fear of God, but assumes for itself the

right to do as it pleases [James 4:13; Prov.12:3;
28:26]. The second claim /97/ is false humility
and false wisdom. It pretends to honor God
and to be nothing by itself. Yet, it cannot deny
itself but seeks its own more and more. This is
utter foolishness and arrogance in the sight of
God who tests the depth of man's heart and searches
out subtle and open sins [Ps.7:10].

Whoever is unable to weigh these contradictory
statements, cannot learn anything thoroughly in
the school of the Spirit. For anyone who does
not know himself and what he can and cannot do,
the same is unable to gain true knowledge of God
[Jn.3:12; Wisd.9:16].

In short, the more a man seeks himself and
his own, the more fully he is assured by God's
Spirit in his heart and conscience that he does
wrong [Wisd. 12:23]. He who would lose himself has
done his best.. Of course, we cannot do any good of
our own making [II Cor. 3:5], except for the Word
that has come unto His own (i.e., unto all creatures), setting us free and making God's children
of us, if we believe Him [Jn. 1:12].

Of Man's Free Will Which Is One With God's Will

CHAPTER VIII

To believe is to obey God's Word--be it unto death
or life--in the sure confidence that it leads to
the best [Heb.11:1]. Whoever does that, cannot
possibly go astray, even though he may err. He
fulfills the Law of God to the highest degree,

even though he may break it. He seeks the best of
all things in heaven and on earth whether he
experiences good or ill; therefore he does not
need a law any more [I Tim.1:9]. He has become a
law unto himself [Rom.2:14]. He is fully free
not to do it unless it be of some avail [I Cor.6:12].
He is one with Christ as Christ is with the Father
[Jn.17:21]. Therefore whoever speaks ill of him,
speaks ill of the Law and of the Word of God which
teaches him all he does [James 4:11; Jn.14:10;
I Jn.2:3]; for of his own strength he can do nothing
other than what he sees the Father do [Jn.5:19].

Thus he is able also to evaluate whether all
his action is good; this does not mean that he is
perfect and without afflictions [Phil.3:12ff]; he
can find in his flesh a great deal of opposition
to the Spirit [Rom.7:14ff]. But /98/ he also
knows that it is truly well with him there [Rom.8:28],
and he is content in the grace of God [II Cor.12:9].
He prays daily for forgiveness of his sins [Ps.32:5]
even though he seeks after the perfection which
he has partly attained [Phil.3:12ff]. Therefore
the Lord has accepted him and is counting him
among the perfected. He lets him know in truth
that he has thus chosen and elected him from the
beginning [II Cor.1:22], so that he can say unafraid
and truthfully: "Thou art my father and I am Thy
son" [Rom.8:15f; Ps.89:27].

Of God's Blamelessness Against His Untruthful
Accusers   Psalm 52

CHAPTER IX

If God the Lord did evil without any distinction, as His unfaithful servants maintain,
He could not punish and judge the world [Gen.18:
16ff], unless He would judge and punish Himself;
this He cannot do. Rather, the enemy of God,
Satan, should be opposed to Him, in the end as
it is happening even now. His mesh of lies should
become revealed to the demise of his dominion
among the elect and also in God's kingdom [I Cor.15].
But thus says the Lord of hosts: "Do you think
that my arm is too short to be incapable of helping
you or that my ear is so ill attuned as to be
incapable of hearing. Your sin alone causes the
separation between you and me" [Is.59:1; Jer.5:23].

He who has ears let him hear; he who has
eyes let him see; open your hearts, dearly beloved,
to the Lord. The Lord says freely and openly:
"I would be merciful and mighty enough to help
you; but you should know that I am just too. If
my strength and mercy are to benefit you at all,
you have to accept my justice first; but you do
not really want to do that. Examine yourselves
well, brothers, and see to it how you are going
to justify yourselves before the Lord when He
will confront you face to face on that great day
of His glory [Ez.20:42].

You say that the Lamb of God has taken away
the sins of the world [Jn.1:29]. How is it then
that your sins are not gone? Yes, you would rather

believe him than try it yourself, as if to say,
"If he has taken away sin in his body, /99/ it may
well be so and I'll be glad to believe it as long
as I am left in peace." O you miserable men;
don't you see what kind of Christians you are?
The Anti-Christ and his whole host of spirits
also confess that Jesus Christ has become man
[I Jn.4:3], just like you. Yet, in their flesh
they do not want to make room for Him, just
like you.

      Therefore I say to you, yet really not I but
the Lord God the Almighty and Just, that He will
make His mercy (of which you now boast) taste
bitter enough. With a rod He shall visit your
transgressions and with plagues your evil deeds
[Ps.89:33]; all the harder, the surer you are
of yourselves [I Thess.5:3].

      Do you wish to have Christ the Son of the
living God for a king [Jn.6:15]; yet he should
not rule over you? [Lk.19:29ff]. Do you want
to be servants of God yet not fear Him?

      Do you want to be children yet not honor
Him like a father? How do you expect to honor
the Father, if you dishonor the Son? [Jn.5:23].
You dishonor the Son if you avoid and ridicule
His way, which He Himself has walked unto life and
on which He desires to lead us too. The Jews and
heathen have dishonored Him from the beginning
[I Cor.1:23]. Not so, dearly beloved, not so:
rather, if you have sinned, honor God as did
Achan [Jos.7:20ff], who allowed himself to be
stoned. You say, "Lord, we have sinned indeed.

Take the sin away from us with Thy righteousness.
Let Thy mercy work in us. For its sake we will
gladly die and be banned, just as long as Thou wilt
not be angry with us." Sacrifice, sacrifice to
justice and hope in the Lord, for you will be
unable to excuse yourselves. In the Lord, I say,
you are able to do so and you could have done it
long ago to endure His work, if you had only
wanted to. For as soon as you truly desire the
good, the Lord is forever ready to give it to
you [Ez.18:21ff; 33:11ff; Wisd.6:17].

On the Trinity, Unity and United Threeness of God

CHAPTER X

     O how gracious is God in His mercy! All day
He spreads out His hand and calls every man unto
Himself. No one answers Him. He rejoices with
unspeakable joy over all [Lk.15:10]. But He is
also very just; we need not fool ourselves on
this. The men who cannot fear and love Him, will
not be loved by God either [I Sam.2; Is.66:15ff;
Ps.5:12; Prov.8:13] even though He loves all men
dearly [Wisd.11:25]. For if He shows love to the
one who resists Him, /100/ He would do the very
thing which He forbids us to do, namely, to throw
holy things to the dogs [Mt.7:6]. This is impossible for Him.

     Get up then, all who sleep so long [Eph.5:14],
that the evildoers may not attack you unawares
[Jer.6:19]; for the Lord is mightier and stronger
than all His enemies [Is.42:13]. Heaven and earth
will pass away in order that His mercy and justice

may be fulfilled [Mt.24:35]. The Lord has sworn
it Himself; it must come true; come what may.
"All knees ought to bow before me, says the Lord
and all tongues shall swear by me" [Is.45:23;
Rom.14:11; Phil.2:10f]. God's good will must
and shall come to pass [Job 23:14; Ps.115:12; Is.
46:4; Wisd.12:16], but the evil tongues of all
His enemies must come to nought and perish [Ps.1:5;
112:10].

Of the Abomination and Idolatry of Ecclesiastical
Pomp without the Worship of God in Spirit and
in Truth

CHAPTER XI

At this point we must needs examine ourselves as to whether we seek the kingdom of God
in righteousness and truth [Mt.6:33]. Let us
rejoice in God [Is.1:16f; 66:2]. We must allow the
Lord to work and reign in us. He will teach us
His wondrous ways [Ps.26:3]. But we boast in our
faith without really knowing what faith is. Thus
it is with all our works and ways: they are not
heavenly, after the spirit, but earthly, after
the flesh [Rom.8:9ff; Phil.3:18].

All our disputing concerns wife and children,
clothes and goods, eating and drinking, wood and
stone, wax and oil, water and wine, bread and
meat and similar outward things. How can that be?
Is our life no more than eating and drinking,
debauchery and wantonness in a heathen manner,
even at its very best? Therefore the Lord your
God says: I will not have any part of your

celebrating and sacrifices. Take away from me
your flesh and bread and all ecclesiastical pomp;
I cannot look at them any longer. They are an
abomination to me [Is.1:10ff; Dan.9:11; Mk.3:28ff].
Indeed, I have not covenanted with your fathers that
they should do these things [Jer.7:22]. I did not
command you to sacrifice calves and sheep so that
thereafter you might be free to serve idols in
injustice and rebellion [I Sam.15:22]. /101/

You yourselves are the calves[Mal.4:2] and the
sheep of my pasture [Ps.79:13]. I desired to have
you for a sacrifice. You do not want to understand
that [Ps.4:6; 51:19; Ecclus.35:1ff; Rom.12:1]. I
did not command you to break bread together like
yelping dogs. I have placed before you my beloved
Son as the right bread [Jn.6:48], that in Him
you too may become such a bread [I Cor.10:17]. As
He was broken for you and as His soul was given
for you in total love, you were to do likewise for
one another [Jn.15:13].

Similarly, I did not order you to wash the
body and leave the soul in the mire or to roll
again in the puddle like washed pigs [II Pt.2:22].
The Lord has called us brothers, unto holiness, and
not to disunity and to such monkey business that
lacks the fear of God [I Thess.4:7].

If you intend to tithe mint, dill and cummin,
you should not overlook the fact that God has
commanded justice, mercy and faith above all
[Mt.23:23; Prov.11:5]. Justice that you may
punish the sinner without respect for the person

[Ex.23:1ff]. Mercy to love your enemies and forgive their mistakes, to the best of your ability
[Mt.18:21f]. Faith, so that you might not take
offense at such judgment before God, but rather
to look for mercy with Him [Prov.3:11f; 13:1,18;
23:26].

     Do you not know that otherwise everything
becomes a yoke of servitude to the world [Gal.5:1]?
Thus it happens that you cannot bring about anything final, if you talk long of the elements of
this world, i.e. outward order; for whatever you
bring about passes away like a reed in the wind
[I Kings 14:15; Mt.11:7; Lk.7:24].

     If the foundation of faith is properly laid,
the entire building can withstand wind and water
[Mt.7:24ff]; actually it is laid by God, but you
must see to it that you do not discard it along
with the false builders [Ps.118:22] , and that you
do not persecute along with the cruel dragon
[Rev.12:3] . Look for it where it may be found,
namely, in the temple and seat of divine glory
which is your heart and soul [I Cor.3:16; 6:19;
II Cor. 6:16] . /102/

Of the False Peace which the Scribes proclaim and
of the Peace of God which is to be Awaited despite
Calamity and Fear

CHAPTER XII

     The builders are the entire people of God who
forever build a wall of stubble, hay and wood--a

veritable fool's job [I Cor.3:12].   Then the
master builders, the scribes and false prophets
come along and whitewash the wall with unmixed
mortar [Ez.13:14f].

They say thoughtlessly and without making
any distinctions (since they are unclean animals
who are not cloven-footed and who do not chew
the cud, [Lev.11:2ff]), "Peace, peace; simply believe
and you are accepted and everything is in order
[Jer.6:4: 8:11; 14:13f; 23:17]."

O you miserable little people; how readily
you entrust your soul to dangerous foxes [Ez.13:4;
Canticles 2:15] ; but you do not trust even for
the smallest bit of bread, the shepherd and
guardian who can protect you. They mislead you,
my people, says the Lord, by flattery and smooth
talk; they spoil the direction of your path [Is.3:12].
For since you have drunk of the cup of desire of
the great whore [Rev.17:2], it cannot be any
different than for you to taste the bitter cup
of divine wrath also (which he has mixed for all
who have spoiled themselves with the whore),
[Ps.75:9; Jer.25:15; 49:12; Rev.18:3] .

Drink in His name and wait for Him in the
night; He will comfort you wonderfully in the
morning.

CONCLUSION

This is the testimony of Jesus Christ which
He has revealed to His servant in this last time
through the abundance of His grace. He has

ordered that a year of grace be proclaimed to His
people so that the miserable ones may sanctify
themselves to the Lord. But he who on account
of the world foregoes divine freedom, shall /103/
be pinned by the ear to the door of his prison
through Satan his lord in testimony of the fact
that he has of his own volition committed and tied
his obedience to this gate. He shall remain there
to all eternity [Ex.21:6; Dt.15:17].

Seek the Lord, you elect, and you shall find
Him [II Chron.15:4]. Indeed, He Himself has
sought you already; just let yourselves be found
[Lk.15:3ff] for He has already found you. He
stands at the door and knocks. If you open, He
shall eat supper with you and you with Him [Rev.
3:20]. That is precisely it; what He takes from
you, He gives to you first and after that it all
remains His, yet is given to everyone. The God
of Israel is the one who can and will do it; He
has the right to it.

Is.55:1-3

"Ho, every one who thirsts, come to get water;
and he who has no money, come, buy and eat. Come,
buy wine and milk without money and without price.
Why do you spend your money for that which is not
bread and your labor for that which does not
satisfy? Do this one thing and listen to me
and you shall live well and your soul shall
delight in fatness. Incline your ears and come to
me; hear and your soul shall live; and I will make
with you a covenant, the steadfast sure love of
David." Amen.

II.6

H. Denck

CONCERNING GENUINE LOVE
(1527)

Schriften, 2.Teil, pp.76-86

Note:

The treatise here translated appeared in three forms. In the earliest and fullest version, published in Worms, 1527, we have the complete text from which this translation has been prepared. Likely in the same year in Augsburg the treatise appeared jointly with two other tractates, but not necessarily at Denck's instigation. A posthumous publication, known as "Item," contains the first part of the treatise only. The section which deals with the application of love to concrete life situations was omitted.

Current Denck research does not seem to support the view that the pamphlet was intended for discussion at the Martyrs' Synod of Augsburg. Since the tractate appeared in Worms in the printing shop of Peter Schoeffer it may well have been a positive effort on Denck's part to express the motivating force in his own life--not so much in terms of theological debate and acrimonious accusations, but rather in the unified totality of a committed "lover," responsive to the power of genuine love personified in Jesus Christ.

As in the Recantation, Denck shows a mature Christian stance. He is duly conscious of his shortcomings and prepared to acknowledge hasty deeds on his part when engaged in hot-tempered debates on the floor of theological opinion and counterargument. He seems to implore his reader to "cast aside all malice and insincerity" and to live peaceably and in the love of Christ "which constrains." Denck emerges as a true pacifist

whose ideal stance is clearly delineated in the
second part of the treatise. The pamphlet has
rightly been considered by some as making explicit
the interrelationship of inner and outer baptism,
an idea that was implicit in the 1525 <u>Confession</u>.

Concerning Genuine Love, etc., 1527

Love is a spiritual power by which one is
united or through which one desires to be united
with another person. Where there is perfect love,
the lover does not deny himself to the beloved.
Rather, he denies himself, as if he were no longer
anything and does not count anything a loss which
he may suffer for the sake of the beloved. Yes,
the lover will not be content with anything he
undertakes, until he has had opportunity to show
his love towards the beloved in its highest
expression throughout all dangers. And whenever
possible (as it may well be), the lover would
willingly and gladly die for his beloved, if thus
he could benefit her.

Yes, a lover is so wanton, (if one might say
so), that he would even die in order to please his
beloved, even though he knows that no good would
come of that, in any case. And the more the
beloved fails to acknowledge the lover's love, the
more he is suffering hurt. Yet, he cannot cease
loving, but must show his love in the highest
measure, even though no one may ever appreciate it.
Thus, where there is genuine love, which is no
respecter of persons, it reaches out and desires
to unite with everyone, in so far as this can happen

without divisions and undue inconstancy; for Love
cannot ever be fully satisfied even by all lovers,
taken together. Yet, even if all lovers should
flee her altogether so that she were unable to
rejoice in them, she is nonetheless so vast in
riches within herself, that she has always had
sufficient, still does today and shall have in
all eternity.

Therefore, Love is willing to deprive herself
of everything, save Love. Indeed, if it were
possible, she would forego Love even for the sake
of Love and become naught in herself so that her
beloved may become what she is. In this respect,
Love hates herself, for she merely desires to be
of service to others and not to herself. If Love
were not willing to sacrifice herself and deny
herself for /77/ the sake of the beloved, it would
be no good. She could not deem herself good because she would then be selfish. Yet she knows
that giving herself so totally for the sake of
the beloved is good. Therefore she cannot hate
herself. Rather, she must love hersrlf, not for
her own sake, but for the sake of her goodness.

Of such Love a little spark may be detected
in many a man; more in one, less in another. Unfortunately, it has been extinguished in almost
everyone in this our generation. However, one
thing is certain (since Love is spiritual and all
men are carnal), this little spark, however small
it may be in a person, does not come from men but
from the source of Perfect Love. This Love is God
who cannot create Himself although He has made all

things; who cannot destroy Himself, although
He shall destroy all things. He is eternally
immovable (impassable). He must love Himself,
since He is good, so that He receives from within
Himself and gives birth to Himself eternally;
who disregards Himself utterly on account of
those who are in need of Him to the extent that
He desires to be nothing at all (if that were
possible) on their account.

    Such Love could not be comprehended by flesh
and blood but for the fact that God demonstrates
it in some people who are called godly persons
and children of God, because they take after God,
their spiritual Father. The more fully such Love
is demonstrated, the more fully it may be known
by men; and the more it is known, the more Love
is practiced. Therefore it has pleased the eternal
Love that the man in whom it was most fully
revealed, ought to be called a redeemer of his
people. Not that it is possible for men to
redeem anyone, but rather because God is so
perfectly united in Love with this man that
every divine deed would be His deed and every
act of suffering of this man would be reckoned
God's suffering. This man is Jesus of Nazareth
who has been promised in Scripture by the true
God, a promise now fulfilled in the fullness of
time, as has been publicly demonstrated in Israel
by the power of the Holy Spirit with every deed
and activity which is Love's just due and pre-
rogative [Lk.4:14].

    Thereby we recognize in this time of love-
lessness that this promise has indeed been

fulfilled in that we know Love of the highest
order and are sure, by the power of the Spirit of
God that God's love toward man and man's love
toward God cannot be manifest in a better way than
in this Jesus in whom God had such compassion
with the world that he was willing to forego all
justice in dealing with our sins, provided we did
not disdain it. This has been amply shown in
the humanity of Jesus, but not as coming from men,
but as taught by God. To wit, man is to stand in
the highest /78/ degree of love toward God and as
far as is possible he should help his neighbour
toward this aim also, so that he too may know
and love God. Therefore, he who desires to know
and attain to genuine Love, cannot receive it
earlier or more readily than through this Jesus
Christ. Indeed it cannot be recognized and known,
except through Him. This is not to say that salvation is tied to flesh and blood, time or place,
but only that it is not possible in any other
way. For as no man can be saved except through
God, so God cannot save a single man outside of
man himself. All those who are saved are of
one spirit with God. But He who is the most
perfect in this love, is also a forerunner of
those who are to be saved. Now, He did not come
here on His own, but it has pleased God at all
times that men should obey and follow all those
for His name's sake who teach His will. The better
one teaches His will, the more readily one should
follow Him. But no one has taught it more perfectly
and better than He who has also executed it most
perfectly, namely Jesus, whom God has sent so
that He might lead Jews and heathen alike out of

their spiritual prison. However, now in this
last age not only Jews and heathen, but even those
who have accepted Him, oppose Him. All those who
have sought and found the way of God have become
one with God, but this very one who has never
faltered in God's ways, has never become separated
from God but has from the very beginning been one
with God in the spirit. Even though He was born
in time, according to the flesh and has been
subject to all human frailty, except for sin.

For this reason it is written and said that
everyone who will be saved, must be saved through
this Jesus, if he is to see the perfection of
the spirit which is the only goal toward which
all who seek to be saved, must look[Acts 4:12].
The less someone looks to this, the more he will
fall short of salvation; the more closely one
comes to this goal, the more he has escaped condemnation. Whatever this love has done and taught,
is truly honorable and good; apart from this,
nothing is honorable and good. Whoever truly knows
what is right and good, but dares teach something
else, however good it may be, would gain nothing
by it but evil. Thus it is with the works and
teachings of Moses, David and any other of the
patriarchs. However good they may have been, at
the point at which this love, which is Jesus,
surpasses them with something better, they must
be considered evil because of the better teaching.
Indeed, they are evil, if one looks at what they
are still lacking, and might well be better.
Thus the zeal of Moses in killing the Egyptian who
had harmed an Israelite was in some sense good
in that he was zealous for the right against the

wrong [Ex.2:11ff]. But if Moses had known
perfect Love or indeed possessed her, he would
have allowed /79/ himself to be killed in place
of the Israelite, his brother, rather than strangle
the Egyptian, his brother's enemy. Such was the
teaching and Law of Moses, to avenge evil with
evil, to protect the good people by force, to
eliminate evildoers by force; likewise to deal
with usury, letters of divorce, the taking of
oaths and such like; considering the uncouth
people of Israel out of whom God intended to
create and bring forth a new Israel, this was
fairly good teaching and law. But had it been
possible for someone other than Jesus to bring forth
the perfect teaching and love, and had the people
been fit to accept these, the former love would
have had to make way so that anyone who might
have resisted or spoken against the new, would
have had to acknowledge the former teaching as
evil and worthless. It is quite clear from this
why it is written that no one can be justified
before God by the works of the Law [Rom.3:20]. For
the righteousness of faith, acceptable to God,
ought to and must exceed by far all works of the
Law; it will have to forego all liberties which
are under perfection.

     For this righteousness is willing and desirous
of restoring to God the Lord, everything, which
is, in other words, all we have and are capable of.
The righteousness which comes from the Law, on the
other hand, commits itself to no more than what is
specifically demanded by the Law and it avails
itself of any excuse which it can puzzle out of
and find in the Law. Therefore those who are under

the Law, are called servants since they will do
no more than is demanded by the Law; but those
who are under faith, are called children by God,
since they do for God's sake as much as they are
capable of, which is always more than can be
worked out in so many words. For this reason
then, they have this privilege from God not to
have a contract or a stated law, except to love
Him; just as a servant, according to the contract
of his lord, has to rise every morning at four or
five and cannot lie down at night until nine while
a son rises and lies down as he pleases without
[benefit of] the law. But he stays with his
father in all dangers, even unto death, whereas
the servant moves away, God willing, whatever may
befall his master.

Therefore, a servant cannot stay in his
master's house forever, nor can he be saved and
enjoy the peace of his master, unless he become a
child or a friend of the child (kindsgenoss), so
that he would not have to go by a contract or
look to his wages but only upon ways to please
his master whenever possible and in the very best
way. This is not to say that the contract which
the Lord made with His people Israel through the
Law of Moses is wrong. It would be wrong to them
only who oppose the Lord while He is intent on
showing them something better still through Jesus,
His first-born after the Spirit, which would not
be against the contract at all, /80/ even though
it may appear to be. For in this way all servants
are hired, to be faithful and well inclined toward
the Lord; as it is written very succinctly in the

Law, to love God with all one's heart, soul and might (i.e. with everything one has and is capable of) [Deut.6:5] . Against this, Jesus has never taught or acted; rather, all His teaching and His deeds aim toward this goal and purpose. Therefore, according to His teaching, eternal life with God is promised to all those who follow Him. Of this very little, indeed, is found in the letter of the Law for the simple reason that servants (as stated above), do not remain in the house forever, but only for a little while.

One might object now by saying that it is ordered that nothing should be added or taken away from the Law. This would imply that it is not seemly to elevate the Law in Love thus relaxing customs and disregarding them. This ought to be carefully considered, for Love is the sum of the Law and no one can too highly regard or understand it or carry it out. He who daily improves in Love, does not thereby add anything to the Law, but simply fulfils it. Love consists in this, to know God and love Him and to learn to lose for His sake and hand over to the Lord all creatures which may be pleasing to man in the flesh. And on the other hand, to accept and bear all things in the love of God which are displeasing to the flesh. From all this it becomes clear now that there is no more than one Love in the old and new Law (as it is called), except of course in the new Law this Love has been made known and shown to the people of God through Jesus the helper. Therefore the old Law proved to be a servanthood because of the ignorance which men still had. Nonetheless, God caught up some of

them as children that they may thus be bidden
to serve. Therefore also the sign of the covenant
which was circumcision, had been given before there
was any need for it, so that all those who came
from the seed of Abraham might be made subject
to the Law, whether they were willing or not.
But the new Law is a sonship in that all who are
under it, do not need to be brought to it by any
man, but alone through a gracious God; and by a
faithful Father they are drawn up and born in their
very souls in that He makes known to them His most
cherished will which is Love itself, brought forth
in Jesus and proclaimed through the Gospel of His
glorious resurrection and still to be proclaimed.

Therefore, Baptism, the sign of the Covenant,
is to be given and not to be denied to any of
those who by the power of God have been invited
to it through knowledge of genuine Love and who
desire /81/ such Love and agree to be followers.
Nonetheless, they are not to be compelled to stay
in this Love by any other fellow of the covenant
and co-heir (unless Love itself compel them), as
is written in the Psalter [possibly Ps.110:3 a]:
"Your people shall be there of their own accord."

But to disregard the customs of the Law is
a freedom permitted by Love and not a commandment.
For though it happened at times, that even the
holy patriarchs had to break these on occasion,
yet without harm to them, one cannot say therefore
that anything other than Love excused them [I Sam.
21]. For this reason Jesus who is this genuine
Love, was silent on that score and neither
commanded nor forbade any of these as if He

wanted to intimate that one may come to this Love
without any of the customs [Mt.12:1ff among others].
He who is not in this Love, gains little value from
customs as such; but he who knows this Love and
has her, is to practice and follow the customs,
as did Jesus Himself.   Therefore it is not necessary
to teach heathen the customs of the old dispensa-
tion, if one preaches to them the Gospel of Love.
For whenever they accept Love, they shall also
learn to conduct themselves within the customs,
wherever this is necessary. It is not necessary
either to hold these up to the Jews, if one intends
to preach Love to them; otherwise the building
up of Love might lead to her destruction. Thus
Love permits her friends to be free of customs in
that they love the Father truly as children, even
though at one time they may have been under a
contract as a servant under his master.

     Now one may be inclined to ask: Why does
Love forsake old customs, putting others in their
place, such as Baptism and the Lord's Supper?
Answer: Merely as a testimony and remembrance
by which the children witness among themselves
and recall from what and for what end they have
been called, namely out of the world to God to
serve Him throughout their lives in holiness and
righteousness, as Zechariah the Baptist's father
says [Lk.1:74ff] . Holiness means to have separated
oneself once and for all from the evil world and
from all filth of the flesh to serve God the Lord
only. This is indicated and witnessed to by water
baptism because in it one declares the old life
to be wicked and desires henceforth to walk in

the new life. Righteousness is to give everyone
his just due, as stated above. Now, one owes God
the Lord everything one has and is capable of in
body and soul, honour and possessions, therefore
everything must be risked /82/ and given up to
the ultimate destruction, for His name's sake. It
should go like this with all children, as it
happened to the first-born Son that He might be
transformed into our nature. Therefore, we should
break bread, one for the other, as He has become
our bread, having been ground into one food and
made our cake. Of all this we are reminded in
the breaking of bread.

Therefore, one breaks bread frequently, but
is baptized only once. For the beginning of the
new covenant happens but once, even though it may
be transgressed and sought after again. As a
child is born of its father but once, even though
it may run away and return; it remains nonetheless
the father's child and is in no need to be born
once more. But the fulfilment of the covenant
which is righteousness must be continuously practiced and carried out. But these customs are not
established so that no one may be saved who does
not keep them, but rather that they be kept in
true earnestness wherever they are observed. For,
however simple and foolish this may appear to the
world, the Lord will not have it despised. Therefore He Himself has set an example so that he may
fulfil all righteousness from the smallest to the
greatest [Mt.3:15]. By this He also intended to
show that nothing is so bad, that something
precious could not be found in it.

This is a summary of the teaching of Jesus
Christ by which all quarrelling that might arise
in the name of truth may be settled for anyone who
understands it thoroughly and desires with all his
heart to comprehend it. He who teaches something
which he has not received through Love, i.e., something which has not been built on this foundation
should not try to justify it before Love. He who
knows this foundation, yet teaches differently,
cannot defend it before Love, even though he may
seek to do so in the name of Love as if he had
done it for her sake. It will be of no avail to
him, for the children of Love are not to do anything against Love in her own name. In this, one
needs all the wisdom of the wise; in this all
friends of God are in need of Love so that they
may not put man's love ahead of the love of God.
For he who loves someone other than through God's
truth and Love, hates him; but he who hates anyone
for the sake of God's Love, loves him more than
the other. But one cannot continue to hate someone for the sake of Love except to punish him
earnestly. And should he be unwilling to accept
this, he is to be avoided despite great pain in
one's heart. In this is found the separation of
the children of God from the children of the world.
This extends to the ban or exclusion of false
brothers also, which has to be truly and totally
done in the name of genuine Love lest one were to
deny the beginning of the covenant of the children
of God which is holiness /83/ and separation
from the fellowship of the world. And this takes
place through baptism, as indicated above. From
all this, it is easy to determine how it is with

infant baptism, the swearing of oaths, the ruling
over the evil ones and such like. These things
God has tolerated for lack of anything better in
the world (although He never authorized infant
baptism). But with those who know love or vaunt
themselves as if they knew Love, He does not let
these things happen any more than He lets evil
happen.

That infant baptism is wrong, is amply testi-
fied by truth in this that the first and foremost
business of the messengers of Jesus Christ is to
teach and make disciples for the Lord and to seek
the kingdom, above all [Cf. Mt.28:19]. This we
too are to do. He who baptizes someone before he
is a disciple, testifies by this deed that baptism
is more essential than teaching and knowledge; but
this is an abomination in the sight of God. If,
on the other hand, teaching is more important
than baptism, one ought to leave baptism alone and
pursue teaching. But if one should ever prefer
baptism, one would have to admit also that it is
more important (than teaching); but this is anti-
Christian teaching. Now, if anyone wants to say
that he places teaching ahead for any of those
who are willing to hear it, the same splits the
commission of Christ and tears it asunder as if
he had been ordered to go to the Jews and preach,
but to the heathen to baptize; it is as if one
should baptize Isaac since his Father Abraham has
now become a disciple. Yet it has been commanded
in this way: "Go then and teach" or "make disciples of all nations, baptizing them (viz. those
whom you have made disciples), in the name of the
Father, who has drawn them and the Son, under

whose yoke they place themselves, and the Holy
Spirit, in whose power they are to remain and
fulfil the will of the Father" [Mt.28:19].   To
sum up, just as Christ is Christ before anyone
believes this, so the teaching is right teaching
before anyone is baptized; but faith is not faith,
unless there is a Christ; consequently, baptism is
no baptism, unless there is teaching.

Oaths and solemn promises are not within human
power to keep. Rather, whatever a friend of God
knows to be right, he is to do without an oath
or solemn promise, as much as is within his power.
Whatever he lacks in order to accomplish it, he
ought to ask the Lord in prayer that He may grant
it to him; but he should not vauntingly promise
anything, as if it had to be granted to him. For
whenever a man vows to do things which he is not
capable of doing (and he is not capable even of
adding a tiny hair) it has to be either presump-
tion without any understanding or else hypocrisy
with understanding, i.e. to pretend to be able to
do something when in one's heart one does not
understand at all. /84/ These two explanations
Scripture too has given when it says: "For you
cannot turn a single hair either black or white"
[Mt.5:36] and, "that you may not fall into
hypocrisy" [probably, James 5:12]. Now one may
want to say: Does not God Himself swear oaths;
therefore we too may do so, for it is written:
"Be ye perfect, as your Father in heaven is
perfect" [Mt.5:48]. Answer: If we can be sure
that we are able to keep them, as He was, we may

also swear oaths, as He did. Similarly it would
be with regard to murder, dominion over others,
if we could only do these without revenge or
selfishness, just like God. But this is not the
case. He who was truly able to do these, has not
allowed us to do them, by way of example, until
His own good time[I Pt.2:23]. How much more then
should we forego these gladly and follow Him
through whom we are to come to the Father who
cannot be known by us without an intermediary.

        But no one should really be too hasty with
"yes" and "no" just because this is permitted.
For anyone who assures and convinces another with
"yes" has already sworn, in that he thereby seeks
to anticipate the will of God. Else, one would
become guilty of swearing a false oath if one were
incapable of keeping the promise . But this is
not the case when done rightly, as for example,
when Paul apologized to the Corinthians [II Cor.1:23]
upon finding that he could not come to them again,
contrary to his earlier assurance. All this is
said about the swearing of oaths concerning future
events. He who wishes to testify to something
that has already happened, in keeping with the
teaching of the Lord, should do it modestly and
with as few words as possible; i.e. yes or no.
Anything beyond that has to be accounted for
before God [Mt.5:37; James 5:12]. If someone
has God for a witness of what he says, that it is
yes, let him put it on, as Paul also had done
[Rom.1:9] . But let him be aware that he ought
not to use the name of God in vain, for this too
is forbidden by the Law as well as in the New

Testament, where it is forbidden to swear on
anything [Ex.20:7; Mt.5:34]. To use God's name
as such is not forbidden and has never been evil.
Indeed, Love bids all her children use it so that
He alone be known, loved and praised in all eternity.

        To use force and govern, however, is not
permitted any Christian who seeks to boast in
his Lord alone. For the kingdom of our King is
in the teaching and power of the Spirit alone.
He who acknowledges Christ truly as his Lord,
ought not to do anything which He does not command [Mt.18:15]. But now He commands all His
students not to deal with evildoers any more than
to teach and admonish them toward their betterment;
in case they do not listen, one ought to leave
them as heathen and avoid them; for those who
are outside (these are the unbelievers), are of
no concern to the community of Christ, except
where they may serve them through teaching. /85/
This is not to say that force in itself is evil,
in view of the evil world, for it serves God in
the execution of His wrath. But Love teaches
something better to her children, namely that they
are to serve God in His grace. For it is the
very nature of Love not to will or desire harm
to anyone, but rather to serve others toward
betterment, as much as is possible. He who is
the head of a household ought to treat wife and
children, manservants and maidservants in the
manner in which he desires God to treat him; Love
does not forbid this. And insofar as it is possible to a government to deal likewise, it might
even be Christian in its position. Since, however,

the world can and will not suffer such, a friend
of God should not get into government but out of
it, if he desires to have Christ for his Lord and
Master. He who loves the Lord, does so in whatever state he may find himself, but he should
never forget what is befitting a true lover,
namely to forego all force for the Lord's sake
and not to oppose being subject to someone else
as to the Lord.

Now someone may say: John the Baptist never
forbade or repudiated the soldiers their standing
when they asked him what they should do [Lk.3:14].
Answer: The Law and the prophets were valid up
to John [Mt.11:13]. John, however, did not come
to do away with the Law, for to do that befits
the Light alone, if it is to happen at all. And
John was not the light, but merely a witness of
the light [Jn.1:8]. He who takes away sin, may
also take away the Law,which is the Lamb of God,
Jesus Christ,to whom John pointed [Jn.1:29-36].
He proclaimed the wrath of God upon all who would
not remain within the words of the Law so that
they might change their ways [Mt.3:7; Lk.3:7].
Christ, however, has first proclaimed grace to
these and offered it to them freely in order that
they might live without blame according to the
good pleasure of God [Mt.3:1ff; Lk.4:16ff].

Everything we have written above, flows from
the perfect Love of Christ from which one may
clearly discern who has the spirit of the Lord
[Lk.9:51ff]. He who understands it but teaches
differently, is a true Antichrist; he who does
not understand it, has not yet learned to know

the Lord Christ. And even though the entire world
may not suffer this teaching, this is nonetheless
the comfort of all children of God that their Father
is stronger and mightier than all the world,
together with its prince the devil [Jn.10:29] .
Indeed, He is so faithful that He will not suffer
any hurt to any of those who trust in Him [Rom.9:33;
Is.28:16] . Woe to him who spares the truth in
order to avoid offence, yet wants to be right.
For such is the devil's love with which he blinds
his children and desires to blind the children of
God as well so that they are more afraid of men
than they are of going against God.

     He who wishes to avoid offence in the Lord,
let him first see what the Lord commands so that
he may not fail to do the same for any reason.
/86/ For such a one does not stand on the right
rock, but in fact has stumbled against the rock
[Mt.5:19; Rom.9:32f].

     The one who teaches a commandment of the
Lord and then abrogates it is the one who truly
offends. In other words, he himself does not
do it and allows others not to do it either; therefore he will be called least in the kingdom of
heaven. But what will the one be called who
abrogates many or all the laws he teaches? He
who teaches in the name of the Lord must not
forget that he also ought to be a student of
Christ; but he who is a student of Christ should
not do anything without permission nor should he
fail to do according to the Master's bidding.

     O you who thirst after Love, seek Love while
she may be found, for God the Lord offers her free

of charge to all who desire her with their hearts.
He who desires her, prepares for the wedding and
even though he may have no wedding gown, the
bridegroom will provide it for him, unless of
course he withholds it from him because he feels
ashamed; but woe to him who comes to the wedding
in the old dress, even though penance may already
have been done for it [Mt.22:11ff].

-----Finis-----

III.7

H. Denck

RECANTATION
(1528)

<u>Schriften</u>, 2.Teil, pp.104-110

Note:
     This document was written during the last
weeks of Denck's life. He had arrived at Basel
during the month of October 1527. In mid-November
he died there. Apparently urged on by Oecolampadius
to write a clarification of his position, Denck
wrote this summary of his beliefs under ten
separate headings. The editor obviously provided
the main heading (see H. Denck, Schriften, I. p.39
and II. p.18ff).

     Fellmann rightly notes that Denck has not
really revoked anything. The pamphlet is a
recantation only in that the underlying mood is
one of futility. Denck is aware, it seems, that
his work in the cause of Anabaptism has been in
vain. He returns, as it were, to his own brand
of religious individualism.

Hans Denck's Recantation

Concerning the
following Ten
Articles
1. On Scripture
2. On the Recompense of
   Christ.
3. On Faith
4. On Free Will
5. On Good works
6. Sects
7. Ceremonies (Rites)
8. On Baptism
9. On the Lord's Supper
10. On Oaths

The spiritual man judges all things [I.Cor.2:15]

Protestation and Confession
concerning certain doctrinal points on which Hans
Denck (shortly before his death) has made himself
explicit in further exposition.

I wish upon all those who seek the way to
salvation in Christ Jesus, ears to hear the will
of His heavenly Father through Him. /105/

I am fully content to have every possible
disgrace and shame fall upon me, provided God is
honored thereby; for He is forever worthy of
honor and love. However, at the moment I began
to love Him, I fell in disfavor with many people;
indeed, the more I progressed, the more disfavor
I encountered. To the extent to which I zealously
strove after God, people zealously strove against
me. I must freely confess at this point that I
strove with a great deal of ignorance. Because of
this many people may have opposed me who otherwise
would not have done so. God alone knows that. I
do not intend to accuse anyone nor do I want to
excuse anyone, although I much prefer to do the
latter (by God's grace). I have been greatly
maligned and accused by some to such an extent
(may they render account of their deeds before
God) that it is difficult even for a kind and
humble man to restrain himself. On this account
I am writing the present pamphlet, in order to
justify myself on the counts   unjustly
levelled against me and to confess the things in
which I have found myself to be errant or imperfect.
Through God's grace I am willing to do the one as
well as the other. Indeed, should I find that I

alone am at fault, I shall willingly ascribe all
the blame to myself. It hurts me in my inmost
heart that I should be at odds with many a man
whom I should acknowledge as none other than my
brother since he worships the very God whom I
worship and honors the very Father whom I honor,
namely, the one who sent His Son as Savior into
the world. I shall therefore, God willing,
attempt as best I can not to have my brother as
my antagonist, nor my Father as judge. Rather, I
shall endeavor to be reconciled with all my
brethren [Mt.5:25].

     Whereupon I beg them for God's sake to for-
give whatever I may have done against them without
intention or knowledge. I am further prepared to
disregard all mischief, damage or shame which
they may have caused me and I shall never
seek revenge.

     In order that this my desire may find a
hearing with them, I have attempted to reveal
my thoughts as far as possible topic by topic
so that they might recognize where I have been
misunderstood and what I really intended to say,
even though my speech fell short of expressing
these thoughts properly. /106/

I. On Scripture

     I hold the Scriptures dear above all of
man's treasures, but not as high as the Word of
God which is living, strong, [Heb.4:12] eternal
and free of all elements of this world; for

inasmuch as it is God Himself, it is spirit and
not letter, written without pen or paper so that
it can never be erased. Consequently, salvation
is not bound to Scripture even though Scripture
may be conducive to salvation [II Tim.3:16].   The
reason is this: Scripture cannot possibly change
an evil heart even though it may make it more
learned. A pious heart, on the other hand, i.e.,
one which has a spark of divine zeal, can be
improved by all things. Thus Scripture serves
believers unto salvation and toward the good.
To unbelievers it is unto damnation as are all
other things.

In this manner, a person who has been elected
by God may be saved without preaching or Scripture.
This is not to say that one should not hear
preaching or read Scripture, but rather that none
of the uneducated would be saved because they
cannot read and many an entire city or country
[would be lost] because there is no preacher who
is sent from God.

II. On the Recompense of Christ

Through His suffering Christ has made satisfaction for the sin of all men. Otherwise no man
could be saved, for none can perceive this save
he who has the Spirit of Christ who equips and
prepares the elect with the same mind which was
in Christ Jesus. He who depends on the merits of
Christ, but continues, nonetheless in a carnal,
animal-like existence, holds Christ in utter disregard, not unlike the heathen in by-gone days who

regarded their gods in such a way. This is a
blasphemy of which the world is full. Yet, he
who believes that Christ has liberated him from
sin, cannot be a slave to sin. As long as we are
in the old life, we do not yet truly believe, nor
do we want to be good and innocent. The resulting
damage is so extensive that it will nevermore go
unrecognized; heaven and earth would sooner pass
away. /107/

III. On Faith

Faith is godly obedience and the surety of
God's promises through Jesus Christ Heb.11:1 .
Where such obedience is not found, the surety is
false and deceptive; obedience must be righteous,
i.e., heart, mouth and deed must be attuned to
each other. There can be no righteous heart
where neither speech nor deed can be felt. Wherever
the heart is not upright, all words and deeds are
utter deception. An evil heart is recognized by
its haughtiness and impatience. A good heart
approves itself through humility and long-suffering.

IV. On Free Will

The one who knows the truth in Christ Jesus
and is obedient to it in his heart is free of
sin, even though he may not be free of temptation.
On the way of God he cannot run any faster than
God gives him strength; whoever runs either
faster or slower than that, lacks truth, obedience
and freedom.

In sum, he who submits his will to God's is
truly free, truly captive at one and the same
time; he who does not thus submit himself is
badly free and badly captive; both together are
liberated for whatever service there needed by
Him whose servant they are.   God does not force
anyone to remain in His service who is not compelled by love.   The devil, on the other hand,
cannot force anyone to remain in his service who
has once known the truth

Thus it is the same, whatever you may want
to call it, free or captive will, as long as you
can discern the difference on both sides.   The
name in itself is not worth the argument.

V.   On Good Works

God shall reward everyone according to his
works [Rom.2:6].   To the evil person He shall mete
out eternal punishment according to His justice; to
the good person, eternal life according to His
loving-kindness.   This does not mean that anyone
deserves anything from God or that He owes anyone
anything if He were to deal strictly and severely
with us.   Rather God recompenses us on the promises
which he has given to us beforehand.   He looks
upon faith and good works, delights in them and
rewards them [James 2:22].   These do not originate
with us.   But we have not in vain accepted the
grace which He has offered us [II Cor.6:1] nor
/108/ have we declined to accept it.   Everything
comes from the one treasure which is precious, the
Word of God, with God from the beginning and made

flesh in the last days [Jn.1:2, 14]. Blessed is
the man who does not despise the gifts of God.

VI. On Divisions and Sects

Hearts which hold high this wondrous deed of
God through Christ and walk in His steps, delight
me. I love them to the extent that I am able to
recognize them. I cannot, on the other hand have
a great deal of fellowship with those who refuse
to hear me, yet will not be silent on controversial
issues, for I cannot detect the spirit of Christ
in them. Rather, they seem to have a perverse
spirit which seeks to force me away from my belief
to theirs, (God beware), be it right or wrong.
Even if this spirit were right and the zeal laudable, it is certainly used unwisely. For a man
ought to know that in matters of faith, things
should be voluntary and without coercion. Thus
I separate myself from some, not because I consider myself better or more just than they, but
because I find a great deal lacking in them in
such matters and I prefer to seek the precious
stone free and without obstruction and, having
found it, I seek to keep peace with everyone
(as far as lies in me). From others again, per-
secutions and such like fears have separated me.
My heart, however, is not turned away from them,
especially not if they are God-fearing. By God's
grace, I do not wish to have anything to do with
error and unrighteousness, [II Cor.6:14] as much
as I am able to discern these, nor do I want to
have fellowship, even though I am among sinners
and those who err.

With such a conscience I anticipate joyfully and
unafraid the judgment of Jesus Christ [I Jn.4:17]
even though I fear men greatly because of my weakness. I do not want to justify myself herewith,
but I know full well that I am a man who has
erred and may further err.

VII. Ceremonies (Rites)

Men prove most clearly that they are human
when they fight arduously over outward elements.
Those who disregard them too much, /109/ offend
unlearned men; those who esteem them too highly,
minimize the honor of God. Ceremonies of themselves are not sinful but he who thinks to gain
salvation thereby, be it through baptism or the
breaking of the bread, has a false faith.

A believer is free in outward things. However, he will seek diligently to do everything in
his power in order that God's honor may not be
diminished through him and that the love of
neighbor be not wilfully disregarded. He who
devotes too much attention to ceremonies does
not gain much; even if one lost all ceremonies,
one does nonetheless suffer no loss. Indeed, it
were better to have none, than to misuse them.

VIII. On Baptism

Baptism is incorporation into the fellowship
of believers. This is not to say that all who
are baptized are believers in the sight of God,
but rather that they alone are recognized as
believers as much as it is possible for one to

recognize this. With children one cannot tell
which is a Jacob and which an Esau. Yet a servant
of Christ ought to be able to differentiate this
above all, after he has learned to recognize
[the differences].

     Infant baptism is a human institution and the
privilege of Christians. No believer will suffer
harm for having been baptized in infancy. God
asks for no other baptism, as long as one holds
to the order which is fitting for a Christian
community; if this is not the case, I do not know
what God will do. Let him who baptizes anew take
heed that he does not labor before he is hired.
For he who is neither called nor commissioned to
teach, undertakes in vain to baptize. For this
reason I would, God willing, stop baptizing altogether, unless I have another call from the Lord.

     What I have done has happened; what I shall
henceforth do, will be of no harm to anyone. The
zeal for the Lord's house has sent me out [Jn.2:
17], but has called back home my reasoning power.
To do right in the house of the Lord is always
good, but to be an ambassador to strangers is not
everyone's task, etc.

IX. On Bread and the Cup, the Lord's Supper or
     Memorial of the Body and Blood of the Lord

     The Lord Christ took the bread during Supper,
blessed it, broke it, etc., [Mt.26:26ff] as if to
say: I formerly said to you that you are to eat
my flesh and drink my blood, if you are desirous
of salvation [Jn.6:54]. He thereby pointed up how

it /110/ is to take place spiritually and not in
the manner in which flesh and blood understand it.
I here put forth the same, that you are to look
upon this bread and wine. For as this bread is
the body's sustenance, if broken and eaten, so my
body will refresh your souls by the power of God,
if it is presented, broken and eaten spiritually
(which means to know and believe).

Similarly, as this wine refreshes and quickens
the heart of the man who drinks it [Ps.104:15], so
shall my blood which I shed for you through the
love of God, quicken you [Jn.6:63] and make you
joyful and zealous in love, if you consider it in
order to become fully one with me, that I remain
in you and you in me, in the same way in which
food and drink mingle to some degree with the
human body.

X. On Oaths

The Lord Christ says: You shall not swear
[Mt.5:34]. He also forbids anger [Mt.5:22], judging,
[Mt.7:1] and to call anyone a fool [Mt.5:22]. Not
that these are wrong in themselves, but rather that
the flesh be not given room nor cause to use such
and to glorify God at the same time, for these are
only misused, all appearances to the contrary.

In this manner everyone uses the oath as if
a promise is not sufficient. Often one binds
oneself by an exchange of promises, apart from
the fact that such is openly against Christ, without light-hearted and thoughtless daily swearing.
He who has the mind of the Lord, however, promises,

swears or confirms nothing other than what he can
do with a good conscience, namely, the things to
which he is obligated by the teaching of Christ,
that is, not to steal, not to kill, not to commit
adultery, not to take revenge and the like [Mt.19:
18]. No one can make such promises other than by
the grace of God, and that not in reference to
what he will do, but rather pertaining to what he
should like to do, so that there be no false pride.

In sum, what one can say truthfully, he can
confirm with God much more readily than with men,
such as the raising of hands and the like, call it
an oath or not. It was not Christ's intention to
forbid such. Paul says: I call on God as my witness upon my soul [II Cor.1:23], as if to say:
God may punish my soul if I do not speak the truth.
And this is none other than to say in our language:
This or that I will or desire to do, God being my
helper; that is, if my intention is not truly thus,
God will not aid me, etc.

IV.   Appendix

<u>PARADOXA</u>
HE WHO TRULY LOVES THE TRUTH
(1526)

<u>Schriften</u>, 2.Teil, pp.67-74

Note:
    Compared with Sebastian Franck's _Paradoxa_
Denck's collection is rather modest. Not only in
volume but also in scope, Denck limited himself in
his attempt to score an important point with
regard to the use and understanding to which
Scripture should rightly be put. Franck produced
280 paradoxical statements which range over a
fairly large field of theology and philosophy.
Denck is content with forty pairs drawn from the
Old and New Testaments.

    Undoubtedly Tauler's influence determined
largely the scope and direction which Denck took.
The Reformer is intent on demonstrating the
higher spiritual unity which must be discovered
if one is to understand Scripture aright and
find in it the genuine path on which to walk.
This strand in Medieval mysticism found a place
in the work of Erasmus. Through his _Ratio_, Denck
as well as Franck must have been led to examine
the "contradictions" of Scripture. A. Hegler
noted in a discussion of Franck's Latin paraphrase
of the _Theologia_ _Deutsch_ (A. Hegler, "Sebastian
Franck's Lateinische Paraphrase der _Deutschen_
Theologie," _Tuebinger_ _Universitaetsschriften_,
1901, p.118, n.1) that both Franck and Denck
often use the very same examples which can be
found in Erasmus' work.

    We offer this translation because it affords
an interesting key to Denck's Scripture principle
and suggests perhaps an often superficial treatment of Scripture. Many of the "opposites" are not

truly such, if the excerpted passage is seen in
its own context. Nor can a text without commen-
tary be taken in evidence for one view or another.

The passages quoted from Scripture by Denck
have been rendered in a form as close to the
German original as possible, in order to preserve
the vivid and forceful juxtaposition of antitheti-
cal pairs. For ease of reference we have numbered
each set of opposites by the letters a) and b).

He who Truly loves the Truth may hereby test
the knowledge of his faith so that no one should
exalt himself but instead learn to know from
whom he might ask and receive wisdom.

The fear of God is the
beginning of Wisdom [Prov.1:7]

Hanns Denck

To The Reader:

Brethren, it is said that in days gone by
many sects and so-called heresies (speaking without malice), had grown up. Some of these can be
seen to grow up again in our own day. In fact
among any twenty scholars of one party one will
seldom find two who agree in all aspects of
doctrine. This should never be the case if one
were to heed the only true teacher, the Holy
Spirit. Scripture gives clear testimony to His
teaching. But this happens in such a fashion that

it might appear to those who are not sealed by
the Holy Spirit as if it contradicted its own
words. One can feel this clearly in certain sects
in which every one fights his own case, quarreling
with the others on the basis of certain parts of
Scripture. Such people disregard the fact that
the opponent's Scripture is truthful too. But if
we are to find the ground of truth, these parts
must be held together, compared and integrated.
As long as we fail to do this, there is no end of
quarreling. Two contradictory statements must
both be true. But the one is contained in the
other as the lesser is in the greater whole, as
time is in eternity, finitude (stat) in infinity.
He who leaves an antithesis without resolving it,
lacks the ground of truth. We would be blessed
indeed if we should recognize how little we
actually have. We would then bemoan our poverty,
and hunger after the bread of life, namely the
Christ of God, our Father. He is master over all
famine, but tends to give to the hungry only. For
this reason then, these antitheses (we could have
found a great many more in Scripture), have been
gathered so that, God willing, they may serve to
enrich His own people. Amen.

The following then are forty antitheses:

The First:

a)   Who knows the mind of the Lord? [Rom.11:34]
b)   He has made known to us the mystery of His
     will. [Eph.1:9] /69/

The Second:

a)   Without Him was not anything made. [Jn.1:3]
b)   Pride was not made for men. [Ecclus.10:18]

The Third:

a)   God did not make death. [Wisd.1:13]
b)   Fire and hail, famine and death, all these
     were created for vengeance. [Ecclus.39:29]

The Fourth:

a)   He who comes to me I will in no wise cast
     out. [Jn.6:37]
b)   Thus it does not depend upon man's will or
     effort, but on God's mercy. [Rom.9:16]

The Fifth:

a)   Thou abhorrest none of the things which thou
     hast made. [Wisd.11:24]
b)   Jacob I loved; Esau I hated. [Rom.9:13]

The Sixth:

a)   God did not repent of His gift and grace.
     [Rom.11:29]
b)   I repent of having made Saul king. [I Sam.15:11]

The Seventh:

a)   I am not come to judge the world but to save
     the world. [Jn.12:47]
b)   For judgment I came into the world. [Jn.9:39]

The Eighth:

a) If I testify on my own behalf that testimony
    is not true. [Jn.5:31]
b) If I testify in my own behalf that testimony
    is true. [Jn.8:14]

The Ninth:

a) I can do nothing of myself. [Jn.5:19]
b) No takes my life from me; but I give it of
    myself. [Jn.10:18]

The Tenth:

a) Those whom He called He also justified.
    [Rom.8:30]
b) Many are called; few are chosen. [Mt.20:16]/70/

The Eleventh:

a) For who can resist His will? [Rom.9:19]
b) You have always resisted the Holy Spirit.
    [Acts.7:51]

The Twelfth:

a) Everyone who asks, receives. [Mt.7:8]
b) You ask, but you receive nothing. [James 4:3]

The Thirteenth:

a) God is no respecter of persons. [Rom.2:11]
b) Whom shall I look upon but the poor and the
    broken in spirit. [Is.66:2]

The Fourteenth:

a)   Preach the Gospel to all creatures. [Mk.16:15]
b)   Do not throw pearls to the pigs. [Mt.7:6]

The Fifteenth:

a)   By one offering He has perfected all those who
     are sanctified. [Heb.10:14]
b)   I complete in my flesh the full tale of Christ's
     afflictions for His body's sake. [Col.1:24]

The Sixteenth:

a)   I will not be angry forever. [Jer.3:12]
b)   And these will go to eternal punishment.
     [Mt.25:46]

The Seventeenth:

a)   God wills that all men should be saved.
     [I Tim.2:4]
b)   Few are chosen. [Mt.20:16]

The Eighteenth:

a)   God does not tempt anyone. [James 1:13]
b)   God tempted Abraham. [Gen.22:1] /71/

The Nineteenth:

a)   Thou art not a God who is pleased by evil.
     [Ps.5:4-5]
b)   Those whom He chooses, He hardens. [Rom.9:18]

The Twentieth:

a) His tender mercy is over all creatures.
    [Ps.145:9]
b) To whom He will, He is gracious. [Rom.9:18]

The Twenty-First:

a) The broken reed He shall not crush. [Is.42:3;
    Mt.12:20]
b) You shall shatter them like a potter's dish.
    [Ps.2:9]

The Twenty-Second:

a) No one has seen God. [Jn.1:18]
b) I have seen the Lord, face to face. [Gen.32:31]

The Twenty-Third:

a) He who drinks of the water which I shall give,
    will never again thrist. [Jn.4:14]
b) Whoever drinks me will still thirst. [Ecclus.
    24:21]

The Twenty-Fourth:

a) He who overcomes I shall grant to sit with
    me on the throne. [Rev.3:21]
b) It is not in my power to grant to you who
    shall sit at my right, but it is for those
    for whom it has been prepared. [Mk.10:40]

The Twenty-Fifth:

a) Judge not so that you will not be judged.
    [Mt.7:1]
b) Judge justly. [Jn.7:24]

The Twenty-Sixth:

a) In Christ shall all be made alive. [I Cor.15:22]
b) The Son gives life to whom He wills. [Jn.5:21]
    /72/

The Twenty-Seventh:

a) God has put all under unbelief in order to
    show mercy to all. [Rom.11:32]
b) He who does not believe shall be condemned.
    [Mk.16:16]

The Twenty-Eighth:

a) This is my body. [Mt.26:26]
b) If they say this is Christ, do not believe them.
    [Mt.24:23]

The Twenty-Ninth:

a) I will be with you until the end of the world.
    [Mt.28:20]
b) Me you do not always have with you. [Mt.26:11]

The Thirtieth:

a) All He wants, He has done. [Ps.115:3]
b) You have always resisted the Holy Spirit.
    [Acts 11:30]

The Thirty-First:

a) He is Himself the atonement for our sin; not
    for our sins only but for the sins of all the
    world. [I Jn.2:2]
b) I do not pray for the world. [Jn.17:9]

The Thirty-Second:

a) It is easier for a camel to go through the
    eye of the needle than for a rich man to enter
    the kingdom of God. [Mt.19:24]
b) My yoke is easy and my burden is light.
    [Mt.11:30]

The Thirty-Third: .

a) The bars of the earth have encased me forever.
    [Jonah 2:6].
b) Then God spoke to the fish and it spewed Jonah
    onto dry land. [Jonah 2:10] /73/

The Thirty-Fourth:

a) To the just no law has been given. [I Tim.1:9]
b) He who conforms to my statutes and observes
    my laws and walks in truth is righteous.
    [Ez.18:9]

The Thirty-Fifth:

a) The Law entered so that sin may increase.
    [Rdm.5:20]
b) God has commanded no man to be wicked, nor
    has He given licence to commit sin. [Ecclus.15:10]

The Thirty-Sixth:

a) For it hereby comes about that the former
    law is annulled on account of its weakness and
    uselessness. [Heb.7:18]
b) Do we then cancel the Law through faith? Far
    be that from us. Rather, we set up the Law.
    [Rom.3:31]

The Thirty-Seventh:

a) With whatever measure you measure it shall be
    measured for you. [Mt.7:2]
b) Double for her the strength of the potion she
    mixed. [Rev.18:6]

The Thirty-Eighth:

a) I am God and there is no other. I bring forth
    light and create darkness, I give peace and
    cause evil. [Is.45:7]
b) When the devil tells a lie he speaks his own
    language. [Jn.8:44]

The Thirty-Ninth:

a) Why do you provoke God by laying upon the
    shoulders of these disciples a yoke which
    neither we nor our fathers were able to bear?
    [Acts 15:10]
b) The commandment which I give you is neither
    too strange nor too far off. It is not in
    heaven that you should say, "Who will go and
    fetch it for us that we may hear and do it? etc.
    [Dt.30:11,12]

The Fortieth:

a) I desire to harden Pharaoh's heart, says God.
    [Ex.4:21]
b) Pharaoh hardens his own heart. [Ex.8:15; 9:34]
    /74/

To the Reader

      The prophet Isaiah says in the twenty-ninth
chapter: "and the vision of all this (that is,
everything which points to God) has become to you
like the words of a sealed book. Give it to a
scholar and bid him read it and he will say that
he does not know it by heart. Give it to an
ignorant man and he will say, I cannot read."
[Is.29:11f]

      This prophecy has already been fulfilled in
our own day. We can easily test this in above and
similar statements. For we understand the mysteries
of God even less than an ignorant animal. He who
cannot read should go with full confidence to the
only teacher who instructs all learned doctors. He
alone has the key to this book which contains all
the treasures of wisdom.

      O Lord, give whatever Thou wilt and to whom
      Thou wilt. Amen.

      Their folly will be plain to all [II Tim. 3:9].

ENDNOTES

Preface

Page 1. 18 order. Rhegius is remembered as chief
reformer of the city of Augsburg. He shared with Hubmaier
a common Humanist education. * 22 (1527). Williams/Mergal,
Spiritual and Anabaptist Writers, p.131, n.9. Cf. also,
Westin/Bergsten, Balthasar Hubmaier, Schriften, p.399. * 26
direction. Westin/Bergsten, op.cit., p.33f seem to think
that Hubmaier baptized Denck, who in turn baptized Hut
shortly after. This on the basis of a letter by P.Gynoraeus
to H.Zwingli, dated Augsburg, 22 August, 1526. However, the
alleged baptism is open to further investigation according
to W.Packull, "Denck's Alleged Baptism by Hubmaier: Its
Significance for his Origins of South German-Austrian Anabaptism," MQR vol.47 (1973), pp.327-338.

Page 2. 20 English. Whether God is the Cause of Evil
(1526); cf. Williams/Mergal, Spiritual and Anabaptist Writers,
p.88ff. * 32 1527. The actual publication dates range
from 1525-1528; the last one being a posthumous edition of
the Recantation, edited by Oecolampadius of Basel. For
further details, see G.Baring, Hans Denck, Schriften, 1.Teil,
Bibliographie (1955).

Page 3. 10 1500. A.Hege in an unpublished Tuebingen
dissertation (1942) maintains 1495 as the year of birth.
Most other biographers continue to maintain 1500. Cf.
Williams/Mergal, op.cit. p.86 for further details. * 29
were. D.C.Steinmetz, Reformers On the Wing, Phil.: Fortress
Press, 1971.

Page 7. 28 extreme. Cf. Sebastian Franck, Paradoxa,
sections 83-85, 119-123, 248 and frequently elsewhere.
According to Franck the Bible is full of contradictions.
It contains a great deal that is foolish and downright
unworthy of God. See also his Preface to the Paradoxa.
* Schwenckfeld. Cf. Caspar von Schwenckfeld, von der
Hailigen Schrift (1551) in C.S. XII, 417ff. See also
Edward J.Furcha, Schwenckfeld's Concept of the New Man,
(The Board of Publications, Schwenkfelder Church of America,
Pennsburg, 1970) pp.28f, 43f, 137ff and 184ff.

Page 8. 16 Christ. Schwenckfeld frequently returns in
his writings to emphasizing the nature of spiritual fellowship as he conceives it. Cf. C.S. 5.336; 7.234; 8.254;
17.816 and frequently elsewhere. Franck's ideas on the
subject are contained in his Letter to J.Campanus (1531)
and in his Kriegbuechlein. For the former, cf. LCC XXV,
p.147ff. * 23 Supper. E.J.Furcha and F.L.Battles, The
Piety of Caspar Schwenckfeld, (Pittsburgh Theol. Seminary,
Pittsburgh, 1969) p.104ff. Cf. C.S. 3, Document 78.

Page 9. 1 Anabaptist. Williams/Mergal. op.cit. p.87
  * 3 churchmanship. A.Schwindt, Hans Denck: Ein Voer-
kaempfer Undogmatischen Christentums, Schlaechtern/Habertshof,
1924. * 6 respectively. R.Jones, Spiritual Reformers, especially chapter XI; Frederick L.Weiss, The Life, Teachings
and Works of Hans Denck, Strassburg; A.Coutts, Hans Denck
Humanist and Heretic, Edinburgh.

1.1 Confession

Page 13. 10 immediately. H.Denck, _Schriften_, 2.Teil, ed. W.Fellmann, _Quellen und Forschungen zur Reformations_ Geschichte, Guetersloh: Bertelsmann Verlag, 1956. Teil 1 of the same volume, containing a _Bibliography_ by G.Baring, was published in 1955; Teil 3, _Religiöse Schriften_, appeared in 1960. * 12 1525. For a response of the pastors of Nuernburg, see pp.24-35, below.

Page 15. 14 witness. The Son of God said that Scripture testifies; yet the scribes say that Scripture creates faith (Muentzer, _Ausgedrueckte Entbloesungen des Falschen Glaubens_, 1524). Cf. Hinrichs, _Muentzer's Political Writings_, p.35,155.

Page 16. 1 completely. Cf. Genesis 32:32. Yet Mary and Zacharias were utterly dismayed in their fear of God so that the mustard seed of faith overcame faith; this is always accompanied by great fear and trembling. (Muentzer, _Entbloess-ungen_). The text may be found in Hinrichs, _op.cit_. p.33,77. * 14 God. "Even though you may have devoured the Bible, it is of no avail. You must suffer the sharp edge of the plow, otherwise you have no faith at all. May God grant and teach you the same "(Th. Muentzer, _Protestation_, 1524). * 18 Scripture. "If Christ is received thus through the revealed covenant--be it the old or the new--and proclaimed without the revelation of the Spirit, much greater nonsense (verwickelts affenspiel) could arise from it than was the case either with the Jews or the heathen." (Th. Muentzer, _Hochverur-sachte Schutzrede_, 1524, in Hinrichs, op.cit. p.75,74).

Page 17. 18 faith. Cf. Rom.10:17. * 23 nothing. The _Theologia Deutsch_ states this concept as follows: "Take note, the willing and desiring which is directed against God is not in God; for God cannot will or desire against Himself. Therefore it is evil; not good, or simply stated, nothing at all." Ed. Pfeiffer (1900), p.197, line 23.

Page 21. 18 (John 6). W.Fellmann has found four of Tauler's sermons (Corpus Christi Day) which have John 6 as their text. Cf. J.Tauler, _Predigten_ 11, Frankfurt,M., 1826. Erasmus quotes Jn.6 in the _Enchiridion_. Schwenckfeld built an extensive reinterpretation of the Lord's Supper on the same text. Cf. Edward J.Furcha, _Schwenckfeld's Concept of the New Man_, p.107ff. Zwingli (_De Vera et Falsa Religione_, 1525) and Carlstadt in several of his tractates on the Lord's Supper also refer to Jn.6. Cf. W.Fellmann, _Hans Denck, Schriften_, p.25 note to line 20.

Page 23. 5 truth. Fellow prisoners were Jorg Pentz, and the brothers Bartholomew and Sebald Behaim, painters who belonged to the Duerer circle. Cf. Fellmann, II.10.

I.2 Evaluation

Page 29. 18 perfect. Luther teaches a gradual growth in the Christian life. See, for example, <u>Enchiridion Piarum Precationum</u> (1543 ed.) vol V.6: "Not yet have we attained that good which has been set for us, but we are struggling toward it, and now are on the road."

Page 31. 4 Law. Cf. Luther, <u>Deutsche Bibel</u>, WA7.51.
* 8 Law. <u>Ibid.</u>, WA7.134. * 17 in us. <u>Ibid.</u>, WA7.53.

I.3 Submission

Page 37. 2 1526. Cf. H.Denck, <u>Schriften</u>, ed. by W. Fellmann, I. 68; II. 12. * 5 Regel. W.Fellmann insists that
Junckherr von Freyberg (not Freyburg, as Denck has it), was
the son of Paul, of Freyberg, Mickhausen. This Bastian von
Freyberg was citizen of Augsburg around 1526. For most
recent information on Georges Regel, cf. J.F.Gerhard Goeters,
<u>Ludwig Haetzer</u>, Guetersloh, 1955.

II.4 Law

Page 45. 10 sides. Denck here addresses the Anabaptists
as much as he does the Lutherans. Neither of their respec-
tive theological arguments seem to have impressed him as
absolutely valid.

Page 46. 8   Jn.10:1 . Cf. Luther, Deutsche Bibel,
WA 6.367.

Page 49. 11 order. "Therefore has Christ made satisfaction for all the damage caused by Adam in order that the
parts might be related to the whole according to the clear
statement of the holy messenger of God who says: I fulfil
that which is lacking in the suffering of Christ." Th.
Muentzer, Von Dem Gedichteten Glauben, 1524. Cf. the Otto
Brandt edition, 1933, p.131,34ff. * 18 members? "If you
say that Christ accomplished it on his own, you fall far
short of the truth. If you cannot fathom the head and its
members, how then do you think yourself capable of following
in His footsteps?" Th. Muentzer, Protestation, 1524. Cf.
O. Brandt edition, 139,22. * 32 expound the Law. See
Mt.5-7.

Page 51. 11 against him. Ez.18; 33; II Pt. 2.

Page 55. 15   Dt.32:40 . For this reason they (the
commandments) have been issued so that man may see his inability to do good and learn to despair in himself. Cf.
Luther, The Liberty of a Christian Man (1520). W.A. 7,23.
See also Luther, De Servo Arbitrio (1525), W.A. 18,766-767.
* 24 from him. Against Paul Rom.10:8 ."For he (man)
ought to know that God is in him. He can neither be spirited
nor thought away even though one is removed from him by a
thousand miles." Th. Muentzer, Ordnung und Berechnung des
Deutschen Amtes zu Alistedt (1524). Cf. Brandt edition,
p.119,26ff. Elsewhere he speaks of the closeness of God's
Word, thus: "That the Word, upon which true faith depends,
is not a hundred thousand miles away from them." Th. Muentzer,
Protestation Oder Entbietung (1524), Brandt edition, p.141,
26ff.

Page 59 5 half-truth. Obviously, Denck proposes that
one has to give equal value to any two contradictory statements in the Bible in order to find the deeper truth. Failing
to do so, results in half truths only. * 16 through Moses.
"Who curse the O.T., dispute greatly with the aid of Paul's
letters, minimizing the Law to the extreme yet do not really
share Paul's line, even though they are about to burst." Th.
Muentzer, Exposition of Psalm 19 (1524), Brandt edition,
p.146, 21ff.

Page 60. 9 it from? These madly raging stupid scribes figured out in their carnal brains that Jesus of Nazareth could not be Christ under any circumstances because he had been raised in Galilee." Th. Muentzer, Ausgedrueckte Entbloessung des Falschen Glaubens, in C.Hinrichs, op.cit., p.54, 734. * 14 without Scripture. Denck identifies himself with an authority principle which was widely accepted by the Radical Reformers. He sets himself apart from the Anabaptists, however, to whom Scripture was normative and the source of truth. He likewise parts company with Luther and Catholic theologians of his day who would have affirmed the agency of the Holy Spirit but never apart from the testimony of Scripture and from the guardianship of the Church. Cf. W.A. 15.118; 19.219; 43.145 (Scripture alone is to be believed). W.A. 33.276, 304; 46.771f, 780 (Scripture is normative for all life and teaching). Cf. R. Seeberg, Lehrbuch der Dogmengeschichte, IV.1. The Anabaptist view of Scripture may be found in several tractates by Balthasar Hubmaier, e.g., his Von Ketzern (1524), Von der christlichen Taufe (1525), Der Lehrer Urteil (1525-26) and elsewhere in Balthasar Hubmaier Schriften, ed. G. Westin and T. Bergsten, Quellen und Forschungen zur Reformationsgeschichte, vol.XXIX.

Page 62. 10 damage. Cf. Mt.25:14-30 (parable of the talents).

Page 63. 7 Kingdom of God. Denck engages in a neat play on words when he juxtaposes Schriftgelehrte (scribes) and gelehrt zum Reiche Gottes. * 18 case. Marginal note: "He who does not sense the pull of the Father is as uncertain of faith as a reed in the wind Mt.11:7 ." Cf. p.96, below.

Page 64. 30 Zech.7:11 . Cf. also Is.55:5; Ps.94:8ff; Ex.20:15; I Sam12:14f.

Page 65. 8 find Him. Marginal note: "With the perverse, God is also perverse."

Page 66. 4 and laws. This tripartite division (Gebot, Sitten, Recht) may be compared with the traditional categorization of moral, ceremonial and judicial laws for which see Melanchthon, Loci Communes (1521), 4 ET: LCC19:67 . Also see Thomas Aquinas, Summa Theologica, FS 89.4. * 22 unjust. This reflects, in a simplified way, the classical view of the uses of punishment which underlies the Reformers' teaching on the use of the law. See Seneca, De Clementia, 1.22.1; Aulus Gellius, Noctes Atticae, 7 (6).14.

Page 67. 8 other. "You must not act like the Learned ones, reciting a saying here and another saying there, without adequate concern for the total spirit of Scripture." Th. Muentzer, Protestation, in Brandt, op.cit. p.139, 18ff. * 15

Key of David. The Latin reads: Donec aperiet tibi librum
septem signaculis obsignatumquis, habet clavem David, qui
claudit. See also, Erasmus, Enchiridion Militis Christiani
(1501) --Similarly, Th. Muentzer, Von Dem Gedichteten Glauben
(1524) in Brandt, op.cit. p.131,14ff: "He has to wait that it
(Scripture) be opened to him with the key of David upon
his shoulder."

    Page 72. 7 hearts. On the other hand, cf. Th. Muentzer,
Sermon Before the Princes (1524) in LCC vol.XXV, p.61:
"Indeed, it is a mark of the truly apostolic, patriarchal
and prophetic spirit to attend upon visions and to attain unto
the same in painful tribulation."

II.5 Divine Order

Page 74. 7 Strassburg preachers. See Hans Denck
Schriften, 1.Teil, p.36, note 3. G.Baring notes there:
"In CR 8, 1914, p.819.5 Koehler leaves open the question
whether the Divine Order or The Law may have been used as
the basis of the December 1526 Strassburg Colloquy between
Denck, Cellarius and the other preachers of that city. The
pamphlet Was geredt sei seems best suited, however to the
reference in Capito's letter, libellumque suum, quem de
libero arbitrio edidit. This seems to have been overlooked
up until now."

Page 75. 1 elect. "But the godless have defiled her
(Christendom) through the neglect of all the slothful elect."
Preface to the Book of Praises by Th. Muentzer, in Brandt,
op.cit. p.113,9.

Page 79. 23 womb. This is essentially the pre-Augustinian
view of predestination, i.e., God's full knowledge of men's
future merits. See W.Fellmann, p.28n.: "Denck turned against
the Reformation doctrine of Predestination, perhaps against
Luther's On the Bondage of the Will. See also p.27, introduc-
tion to Denck, Was geredt sei, dass die Schrift sagt, 1526.

Page 82. 29 him Jer.23:24 . "For God stands so close to
you that you would not believe it." Th. Muentzer, Sermon
Before the Princes, LCC, vol.XXV, p.64.

Page 88. 17 have free will. Denck undoubtedly refers
to the controversy between Erasmus and Luther whose main
points are found in Erasmus' De Libero Arbitrio sive Collatio
(Basel, September 1524) and in Luther's De Servo Arbitrio,
reluctantly published in December 1525 WA 18.597ff . The
quarrel dates from 1516 at least and is reflected in the
extensive correspondence of Erasmus, especially between
1517-27. From among the pertinent literature on the subject, see A. Freitag in WA 18.551ff; P. Smith, Erasmus,
2nd ed. New York and London, 1962; J.I.Packer and O.R.Johnston,
Martin Luther on the Bondage of the Will, 1957.

Page 89. 11 Spirit. Ler des geysts. Denck uses the term
"School of the Spirit.'" In Schwenckfeld the term "School of
Christ" frequently appears. Both terms seem to denote a
widespread emphasis among 16th century Radicals on true
learning which is best attained in the master-student relationship between the Lord Christ and his faithful students.
In Calvin, Inst., 3.21.3, the phrase more explicitly refers
to Scripture. Cf. Caspar Schwenckfeld, Apologia (1529)
Corpus Schwenckfeldianorum, 3.404.9-18; E.T.: Furcha/Battles,
The Piety of Caspar Schwenckfeld (1971), p.13: "Now for
several years I have totally subordinated myself to my Lord
Jesus Christ after a gracious visitation through Him; with
the aid of the Holy Spirit, I have entered the discipline,

the training school, the teaching of God the Heavenly Father,
presenting myself a living sacrifice." * 13 knowledge of
God. On the two knowledges, cf. Calvin, Inst., 1.1.1.

Page 93. 12 Threeness of God. The text does not bear
out what the title implies. Denck does not enter into any
explicit discussion on the trinitarian understanding of
God. If anything, he affirms the unity of God by reference
to the Scriptures. The divine qualities listed here are
justice, mercy, love and will.

Page 95. 26 of God I Thess.4:7 . "Right baptism is
not properly understood. As a result entry into the Christian
fold has become a monkey business." Th. Muentzer, Protestation
in Brandt, op.cit. p.132, 7. Cf. I Thess.4:7. * 31 for
the person. A common Scriptural phrase, "God is no respecter
of persons," i.e., shows no partiality. See for example
Dt.10:17; I Chr.19:7; Job 34:19; Acts 10:34; Rom.2:11;
Gal.2:6; Eph.6:9; Col.3:25; I Pt.3:17.

Page 97. 8 cud, Lev.11:2ff . "Therein no one opposes
me, then the unclean beasts whose feet are not cloven (as
pointed out in the Law of Moses)." Luther, On Good Works
(1520) WA 6.209.10. * 13 Canticles2:15 . Cf. also Ez.34:23;
37:24; Jn.10:12; I Pt.2:25.

II.6 Concerning Genuine Love

Page 100. 12 omitted. For further bibliographic
references, cf. G.Baring, Hans Denck Schriften 1.Teil,
pp.34ff, 53ff, and 55ff. See also W.Fellmann, ibid, 2.Teil,
p.75.

Page 101. 5 1525 Confession. G.H.Williams, The Radical
Reformation, pp.160ff. * 9 person. According to H.Quiring,
Luther und die Mystik, (1936), Denck's formulation here is
somewhat like Luther's in his Lectures on Romans (W.A.56;
241.5 II 78) "Amor enim vis est unitative ex amante et
amato unum quid constituens." Love is a unitive force,
constituting out of the lover and the loved one thing .
There is undoubtedly here a resemblance to the thought
of pseudo-Dionysius the Areopagite.

Page 106. 17 make way. The text should perhaps read:
"And if there were something better than God, that would
have to be loved more than God." Theologia Deutsch, ed.
Pfeiffer (1900) p.123, line 18.

Page 109. 20 co-heir. C.Krahn, Menno Simons (1936),
p.23 note 53 traces the term for baptism as "sign of the
covenant" and for members of the church as "fellows of the
covenant" through the writings of Melchior Hofmann to a
Strassburg document by Kautz/Reublin of the year 1529.
It would appear from this passage that Kautz/Reublin in
turn borrowed it from Denck. As a result one may take this
document to be the source of these Anabaptist terms Fellmann .

Page 114. 8 teaching. At this point the text in the
collected volume "Item" ends. Yet according to Fellmann
the remainder also belongs to this same treatise although
he does not advance any theory why this should be so,
except of course, for the fact that in some manuscripts
the two sections are found together. The concluding for-
mula (To sum up...teaching) is found verbatim in Hans
Denck's Notes on Baptism for Johannes Bader in Landau of
January 1527, one of the most important check-points for
the dating of our writing. See Denck Schriften (1.Teil,
pp.35, 52).

III.7 Recantation

Page 124. 15 or Scripture. "Now if someone should
neither have heard or seen a Bible all his life he might
well have, nonetheless, by the righteous teaching of the
Spirit an unmistakably Christian faith as did all those
who wrote on Holy Scripture without the aid of any books.
Cf. Th.Muentzer, Ausgedrueckte Entbloessung in Th.Muentzer,
Politische Schriften, ed. Carl Hinrichs, p.36,167.

Page 128. 2 Christ. Cf. I Jn.4:17 "It depends on me.
But the Word of Christ I shall account for with a glad
heart and boldly with no regard to anyone. Toward this,
God has given me a joyful bold spirit which they shall not
dim, I hope in all eternity. M.Luther (1520), W.A. 6.323.

IV. Paradoxa

Page 133. 20 Scripture. For English translation and study of Erasmus' <u>Ratio Verae Theologiae</u>, see doctoral dissertation of Donald B. Conroy, U. of Pittsburgh, 1974.

Page 140. 17 Mt.24:23 . Cf. M. Luther, <u>Die Himmlischen</u> Propheten (1525), W.A. 18,210.34 "since we say that Jesus Christ is in the elements it is saying as much as 'here is Christ' therefore it is false. Right on." Cf. also W.A. 18 211, note 1. Carlstadt had planned fifteen counter arguments. The last of these was to have had the title: "When they now say here is Christ, etc...."

Page 143. 25 all II Tim.3:9 . The last statement is not contained in other available editions.

Scriptural Index

Hans Denck

* = Critical Evaluation of Hans Denck's Confession by the
Nuernberg Preachers (1525).

Genesis

1:27.......78
2:17.......51
3:15.......84
3:24.......68
6:3........85
8:21.......80
11:1ff.....26*
18:16ff....91
22:1......138
32:26......83
32:29f.....83
32:31.....139
32:32......16n
49:10......86

Exodus

2:11ff....106
3:7........78
4:21......143
8:15......143
9:34......143
20:6.......88
20:7......116
20:15......64n
21:6.......98
23:1ff.....96
34:28......22

Leviticus

10.........71
11:2ff.....97
20:9ff.....54

Numbers

16.........71
23:19......86
24:17......86

Deuteronomy

4:6........48
5:26.......44
6:5.......108

DATE DUE